"The best kind of therapy is when it's child doesn't know it's happening. LE fits that bill. The authors have left n developing a systematic social intervention. They provide a comprehensive, step-by-step program with documented improvements in social competence."

—*Lynn Koegel, PhD, Clinical Director, Koegel Autism Center, University of California, Santa Barbara, CA*

"Everyone loves LEGO®—including children on the autism spectrum. But did you know that through playing with LEGO® in a social setting you can draw out autistic children's hidden ability to cooperate with others? Here is a practical guide to making players come together and create together by the sheer magic of LEGO®."

—*Professor Uta Frith, Emeritus Professor of Cognitive Development, Institute of Cognitive Neuroscience, University College London*

"A marvellous book that focuses on using a frequent interest as a way of access. It will be of interest to parents and educators alike."

—*Fred R. Volkmar, MD, Irving B. Harris Professor of Child Psychiatry, Pediatrics, and Psychology, and Director, Yale University Child Study Center, New Haven, CT*

"LEGO® pieces can be used to construct models, but can also be used to construct social skills. LEGO®-Based Clubs will become increasingly popular with children who have an Autism Spectrum Condition as an enjoyable social activity that is actually therapeutic."

—*Tony Attwood, PhD, Clinical Psychologist, Minds & Hearts Clinic, Australia, and author of The Complete Guide to Asperger's Syndrome of related interest*

Engaging Mirror Neurons to Inspire Connection and Social Emotional Development in Children and Teens on the Autism Spectrum
Theory into Practice through Drama Therapy
Lee R. Chasen
Foreword by Robert J Landy
ISBN 978 1 84905 990 9
eISBN 978 0 85700 908 1

Simple Low-Cost Games and Activities for Sensorimotor Learning
A Sourcebook of Ideas for Young Children Including Those with Autism, ADHD, Sensory Processing Disorder, and Other Learning Differences
Lisa A. Kurtz
ISBN 978 1 84905 977 0
eISBN 978 0 85700 879 4

Teach Me With Pictures
40 Fun Picture Scripts to Develop Play and Communication Skills in Children on the Autism Spectrum
Simone Griffin, Ruth Harris and Linda Hodgdon
Illustrated by Ralph Butler
ISBN 978 1 84905 201 6
eISBN 978 0 85700 632 5

Social Enjoyment Groups for Children, Teens and Young Adults with Autism Spectrum Disorders
Guiding Toward Growth
John Merges
ISBN 978 1 84905 834 6
eISBN 978 0 85700 323 2

Secrets to Success for Professionals in the Autism Field
An Insider's Guide to Understanding the Autism Spectrum, the Environment and Your Role
Gunilla Gerland
ISBN 978 1 84905 370 9
eISBN 978 0 85700 724 7

LEGO®-Based Therapy

How to build social competence
through LEGO®-Based Clubs
for children with autism
and related conditions

Daniel B. LeGoff, Gina Gómez de la Cuesta,
GW Krauss, and Simon Baron-Cohen

Jessica Kingsley *Publishers*
London and Philadelphia

First published in 2014
by Jessica Kingsley Publishers
73 Collier Street
London N1 9BE, UK
and
400 Market Street, Suite 400
Philadelphia, PA 19106, USA

www.jkp.com

Library of Congress Cataloging in Publication Data
A CIP catalog record for this book is available from the Library of Congress

British Library Cataloguing in Publication Data
A CIP catalogue record for this book is available from the British Library

ISBN 978 1 84905 537 6
eISBN 978 0 85700 960 9

Printed and bound in Great Britain

Contents

1

Introduction

History and Rationale

LEGO®-Based Therapy is a social development program that has evolved over time as a consequence of ongoing attempts by the authors to provide an effective social development intervention for children with autism spectrum conditions (ASC) and other conditions affecting social competence. The strategies used in LEGO-Based Therapy reflect clinical observation, outcome research, and the influence of an inspiring and persuasive group of children. It was clear from the outset that the participants were enthusiastic and responded generally more positively to this approach than to other traditional forms of intervention, and there seemed to be a fairly noticeable improvement in social responsiveness and social adjustment in a relatively short period of time.

These informal observations were subsequently examined more closely in a series of outcome studies, including one relatively short-term study (LeGoff 2004), a longer term study (LeGoff and Sherman 2006), and then an independent replication study (Owens *et al.* 2008). The initial impetus for developing LEGO-Based Therapy was the result of the scarcity of social development programs with evidence of demonstrated effectiveness for improving social and communication skills for children with ASC and other conditions adversely affecting social development and communication. The term "evidence-based" is often used to refer to treatments or interventions for which there is data-based, published research demonstrating that they are as effective for the problem and the target audience as the treatment approach claims. This is especially necessary for children or other populations of individuals who may have little means to report directly on the effectiveness of the intervention themselves.

Detailed, objective, and replicable records of the successful implementation of a therapy, otherwise known as outcome studies, need to be available before a treatment should be considered evidence-based. These studies should be published in a refereed journal or other peer-refereed publication, which means that colleagues and experts in the field have reviewed the study and found it to be credible in demonstrating the effective outcomes that are claimed. More importantly, these publications can be read and judged by other researchers and clinicians, and can lead to independent replications of the original research, thereby verifying that the method and the outcomes were not specific to a single therapist or group of therapists, or to a specific group of participants. Self-published studies, or manuals which simply describe a therapy approach without outcome research, are often little more than advertising, and may describe interventions which could actually be harmful or, at best, useless. In the mid-1990s, when the LEGO®-Based Therapy model of intervention was first developed, there were very few published descriptions of effective interventions, and virtually none that had replicable outcome results.

The second major reason for the development of this approach was the fact that the few therapy approaches in use at the time often seemed difficult, irrelevant, and un-engaging for the children and adolescents involved. In other words, for most educational, behavioral, and mental health specialists working with children with social development deficits, the existing therapies were neither effective, nor fun.

Although it is often noted that children with ASC tend to be uninterested in social learning opportunities, and have little intrinsic motivation to improve their social functioning (Attwood 1998; Klin and Volkmar 1997; Klin and Volkmar 2000; Strain and Schwartz 2001), there have been very few published studies which provide clear evidence of effective interventions designed to overcome these hurdles (Reichow and Volkmar 2010; Licciardello, Harchik, and Luiselli 2008; Luiselli et al. 2008).

Similarly, children with other mental health conditions or social learning problems (e.g. anxiety disorders, social adjustment difficulties, stigma, childhood abuse/neglect/ trauma, social isolation, physical or sensory disabilities) are also often resistant to participating in group activities with peers (Christophersen and Mortweet 2001; Garber, Garber, and Spizman 1993; Kendall and Hedtke 2006). Often this has been due to anxiety about or unfamiliarity with peer group social situations, and the inherent demands for social competence in those situations (Rapee and Heimberg 1997). The "LEGO® Club" model was developed largely because of the interest and motivation to participate shown by these children who might otherwise be resistant or aloof in social situations with peers. The model clearly required both social interaction and communication with peers, but was also engaging, inviting, and a safe experience for children who might otherwise dread peer group settings (LeGoff et al. 2010, 2011).

A third reason for the development of this approach was the fact that although many children with ASC and other conditions can learn to respond appropriately to social skills exercises in the intervention or educational setting, and can demonstrate appropriate responses in social learning role-play situations when prompted by adults or peers in some settings, the generalization of these skills to new settings and to everyday life was often unsuccessful (Licciardello *et al.* 2008; Howlin *et al.* 2004). They were able to learn the rules and follow the exercises, but they were not necessarily able to execute these skills in social situations outside of the therapy setting where it mattered most. Improving independent social motivation and social competence has been very difficult to demonstrate and document: there has been a persistent absence of self-initiation of social interaction, especially with peers, including a failure to develop age-appropriate peer relationships, that is, friendships (Klin and Volkmar 2000). Children with autistic and other social learning conditions appeared to be able to learn from social and play drills and exercises, and when prompted by an adult could demonstrate the correct behavior in the classroom or group activity, but they were not initiating sustained interaction, communication, or play on the playground or neighborhoods, and they were not making friends (Howlin *et al.* 2004; Strain and Schwartz 2001).

Although there have been a number of published guidelines for social skills interventions for children with ASC (Licciardello *et al.* 2008; Gray 2000; Frea 1995; Quill 1995; Mesibov 1984, 1992; Gray 1994; Gray and Garand 1993), few of these provide much empirical evidence of effectiveness (Swaggart *et al.* 1995; Ozonoff and Miller 1995). In addition, despite the work of a few clinical researchers describing different diagnostic groups and clinical features (Ozonoff and Griffith 2000; Schopler and Mesibov 1986, 1992; Baron-Cohen 1995), there has been little empirical research regarding which therapy approaches might be more or less effective for which problems or conditions. The current treatment literature indicates that psycho-educational interventions should be tailored to the needs and strengths of the individual child and family (Albanese, San Miguel and Koegel 1995; Harris and Weiss 1998; Schopler 1987), but there is still scant data available to guide these treatment decisions. Recently, there has been a significant expansion of ASC treatment literature (Reichow and Volkmar 2010; Weiss and Harris 2001; Quill 1997; Freeman 1997; Koegel and Koegel 1995). Unfortunately, there remains very little empirical data available on the outcomes of these interventions for improving social competence, and even less on the variables affecting outcomes. A comprehensive discussion of the recent treatment outcome literature is beyond the scope of this manual and the reader is referred to the following texts: Luiselli *et al.* (2008); Klin and Volkmar (2000); National Research Council (2001); Schopler, Mesibov, and Kunce (1998); and Harris and Handleman, (1997).

The Development of LEGO®-Based Therapy

The choice of LEGO play materials as the basis for a social development therapy was based to some extent on Attwood's concept of "constructive application," that is, using the child's own interests to motivate learning and change (Attwood 1998, p.96). Attwood and others (Cumine, Leach, and Stevenson 1999; Klin, Volkmar, and Sparrow 2000; Myles and Simpson 1998) described children with ASC as not interested in the need to please their teachers and parents (and therapists), ignoring the usual social pressures to conform to peer groups, imitate peers, cooperate with them, or compete with them. Consequently, many of the techniques recommended for social skill building which utilized adult instruction and modeling have had little impact or, worse, have resulted in robotic attempts at imitation. Although use of external rewards can improve compliance, these gains are usually short-lived, and intrinsic motivation for learning is rarely achieved (Greenspan and Wieder 1998; Heflin and Simpson 1998; Koegel *et al.* 1992; Koegel and Koegel 1992). At the same time, these children often develop singular, obsessive interests and habits, and appear to have limitless reserves of focused energy and drive when engaged in these activities. It has therefore been recommended that children's idiosyncratic interests and/or behaviors be used to promote the learning of social, communication, and play skills (Attwood 1998; Greenspan and Wieder 1998; Koegel and Koegel 1995). Most published studies of social skills interventions have also emphasized the importance of peer modeling, peer interaction, and opportunities to practice social competence with peers (cf. Harris and Handleman 1997; Laushey and Heflin 2000; Pierce and Schreibman 1997).

The initial idea of using LEGO® as a therapy tool in a structured and comprehensive way in order to increase motivation to participate and interact with peers arose from an inadvertent observation. Two of Dr. LeGoff's clients, both eight years old and diagnosed with Asperger's Syndrome, were found excitedly playing and talking together in the waiting room. They had coincidentally brought LEGO creations to the clinic that day, and as one was leaving and the other was arriving, they discovered each other. These two boys had previously shown little or no interest in each other, and had low motivation for social interaction in general. After a discussion with their parents, we agreed to try to work with the two of them together using LEGO as a medium for them to communicate and to motivate them to continue the relationship. Initially it was just the two of them. They brought LEGO constructions to share, or built LEGO sets which were provided.

They were clearly motivated to complete new LEGO sets (the reader may have seen or experienced this phenomenon directly) and cooperated fully with social skill-building strategies such as sharing, turn-taking, making eye-contact when appropriate, following social rules, and using greetings and names. Compliance was not a problem, as long as they were permitted to build LEGO® sets. A key strategy for sustaining interaction involved dividing the task of set-building so that they had joint and interactive jobs to do: one was given the LEGO pieces to put together, and the other the visual instructions. The "Engineer" was required to give verbal descriptions of the pieces needed and directions for assembling them, while the "Builder" followed his directions, collected and put the pieces together. There was much checking back and forth between the plan and the creation.

Roles were then switched so they both had a chance to be "Engineer" and "Builder." Much of this was done through nonverbal communication and required considerable emphasis on joint attention, eye contact, and "mind-reading" (understanding each other's points of view, emotions, interests, and opinions) in general (Howlin, Hadwin, and Baron-Cohen 1999). We also did joint "freestyle" building, in which the two of them had to agree upon a project, the design and materials, and the final shape and color of the creation. This required considerable problem-solving and some conflict resolution. Rules to follow were provided, but the boys were generally left to muddle through on their own as much as possible. Eventually, the two of them developed a relationship independent of the therapy, and started meeting for "play dates" outside of the joint therapy sessions.

Individual therapy continued alongside the joint sessions, allowing for reviews, practicing, and rehearsing skills and problem-solving strategies so that we could implement these in the next joint session. Individual sessions were also centered around LEGO building, which we used as an interactive medium for working on turn-taking, perspective-taking, eye-watching, joint-attention, and question-asking. During the group session, one or the other could be cued about something practiced in individual therapy, such as following gaze, asking social questions, making apologies, or initiating play. The back-and-forth between individual and joint sessions added considerably to the effectiveness of the therapy overall. If something came up in the joint session, for example an unresolved dispute, an inappropriate or annoying behavior, or a frustrating situation that led to an emotional outburst, we would revisit that in individual therapy and work on the underlying skill and frustration tolerance.

Group Therapy: The "LEGO®-Club"

Soon after beginning LEGO-Based sessions with the initial two clients, the LEGO collection of sets and freestyle creations began to grow, and others began to express an interest in using them. The children with ASC and other socially anxious and inhibited children seemed to naturally gravitate towards LEGO, and ignored the other toys and activities that were also provided in the playroom and which eventually went into the storage closet (puppets, paints, sand-tray, dolls, board games, Play-Doh®, etc.). Somewhat surprisingly, the first two LEGO enthusiasts were happy to have others join them. The LEGO creations and paraphernalia, LEGO posters, pictures of the children and their favorite LEGO creations, postcards from LEGO-Land® trips, and LEGO magazines and catalogues soon filled the large playroom.

Eventually, there were seven children in the group. Work with the larger group utilized the same strategies that had been developed with the first two members: collaborative work, division of labor, sharing, turn-taking, cued eye-contact and gaze-following, emphasis on verbal and nonverbal communication, taking advantage of natural opportunities for practicing social support (tearful outbursts were a common occurrence), social problem-solving, and conflict resolution. The groups focused primarily on three activities: repairing and restoring existing LEGO® sets, building new LEGO sets, and doing group-designed freestyle creations.

Once the decision was made to increase the size of the group (which came to be referred to by staff, clients, and families as the "LEGO Club"[1]), there was a need for increased structure, and a consistent set of rules (Kunce and Mesibov 1998). LEGO-Based therapy strategies also evolved, such as LEGO-building contests in which members worked in pairs or teams of three, with a jointly determined project and goal.

For the first time for most of the participants, they identified with a peer group, and began to be motivated by social approval and social status within the group. In order to become a better LEGO Builder, which was associated with increased status with their peers, they needed to learn from them, cooperate with them, solve disputes, and be helpful. Initially we used a formal "LEGO Points" system, in which points were awarded for behavioral, social and LEGO-related achievements which could be traded in for LEGO prizes (small sets, LEGO mini-figures or "mini-figs," etc.). After a period of two or three weeks (sessions were held weekly), the points became inherently valuable, and no longer needed to be associated with any reward, other than the social approval and gratification associated with earning

---

1 The LEGO-Based Therapy groups were referred to by participants, parents, and providers as the "LEGO Club," but this had no relationship with LEGO Corporation's media-based LEGO® Club®. The term "LEGO Club" is used here for historical accuracy. For professional or other media references, the intervention should be referred to as "LEGO-Based Therapy".

LEGO points. Group members continued to follow social and behavioral rules, practiced "mind-reading," solved social conflicts, and exhibited pro-social behavior long after the points became merely a verbal "feather in the cap."

The "LEGO Club" was instantly popular with parents, in part because their children were highly motivated to participate in the therapy. They noticed that their children reminded them about the dates and times of "LEGO Club" sessions, excitedly discussed group activities, and were often devastated when they could not attend a group for some reason. After a few weeks, the parents spontaneously formed a "LEGO Club" support group in the waiting area. They discussed their children, their Individualized Education Plans, the impact on their other children and extended families, the strategies they were using at home, and so on. Some also began to get together socially outside of the group sessions. At the suggestion of a parent, non-ASC siblings were included in the younger groups as role models and "Helpers." They were well-suited as Helpers, as they were familiar with the problems of their sibling, and required little prompting to provide redirection for stereotyped behaviors, or distraction from oncoming outbursts.

Over time, various social skills strategies were included as activities in the group, over and above the ongoing LEGO-Based activities. Some were successful, and some were not—successful and unsuccessful strategies are described in Chapter 5. Eventually, in its initial incarnation (in Dr. LeGoff's private practice in Honolulu, HI), there were nine LEGO social development groups altogether, with members ranging from pre-school to high-school ages, and some members continued to come, forming groups for young adults. Some of the original group members were still participating after seven years (on a social, *pro-bono* basis at that point). Although the style of interaction in the group changed over time, becoming more verbal, and the types of LEGO changed (more sophisticated, complex, electronic sets and computer software games), the group membership remained very consistent. The group members became like family members to each other, and other group members' families became like an extended family. To this day, about 15 years since the start of the first LEGO® groups, many group members and their families remain in touch with each other, and with Dr. LeGoff, via electronic media as well as through established friendships.

Currently, LEGO-Based Therapy is utilized in a variety of settings throughout the US and UK, as well as in Canada, Australia, New Zealand, China, and India. The focus of these groups is the provision of an activity-focused social milieu in which children participate with peers and are coached and supported to improve effective social communication and collaboration. The identification of the group activities as a "therapy," *per se*, for the children, is discouraged. The group is identified as the "LEGO Club," and the child's other interests are highlighted and encouraged, if necessary.

Many participants have limited familiarity or interest in LEGO building as an activity in and of itself, but often have other interests or preoccupations which can usually be quite easily accommodated by the extensive range of LEGO materials and themes. Interest in trains or other vehicles, structures, systems (e.g. numerical, alphabetical, physical, or mechanical), and topics such as meteorology, geology, maps, insects, space exploration, archeology, architecture, zoology, agricultural, transportation, military and construction equipment, Japanese anime and other animation themes, are all potential subjects for LEGO modeling. The range of available LEGO sets with content that suits these interests is almost limitless, and of course, the freestyle creative process (building models of unique design) is literally limitless.

Identifying a child's particular interests or preoccupations is never difficult, and translating these interests into readily accessible LEGO®-building projects is also typically a straightforward process.

For most children, the affinity for the unified system of LEGO and its inherent plasticity in terms of accommodating these different areas of interest is often supported by the peer group within the Club. As one of the first "LEGO Club" participants commented about a peer, on first joining a "LEGO Club": "Dr. Dan, that kid is from my planet." This experience is often a fairly unique and highly rewarding experience for both the participant and their parents. For many, this is the first opportunity they have had not only to explore and express their creative energy in a three-dimensional and accessible modality, but to do so in a socially and culturally sanctioned way, supported by their parents, their adult leaders, and their peers. The price of admission to this highly rewarding activity, however, is to relinquish an entirely self-focused worldview, and accept the requirements of following social conventions and rules of appropriate conduct, participating collaboratively, recognizing and accepting the different interests and idiosyncrasies of their peers, and meaningfully engaging in joint achievement, as opposed to solitary pursuits. Often, this is a frustrating and even overwhelming task: "Why can't I just do my own thing?"

The benefits of the mandate to share materials, to share ideas, to reciprocate efforts, is often elusive and burdensome. Eventually, however, sometimes very quickly, and sometimes very slowly, the participants will express an insight about the benefits of joint accomplishment. The first time a child takes on a daunting LEGO-building task—often with many hundreds of steps—and accomplishes this with their peers in an unprecedented short period of time, they invariably recognize the benefits of having collaborators. This insight is often expressed first to parents, siblings, or grandparents with the use of plural pronouns: "Mom, Dad, look what *we* did today!" There are also expressions of the insight of the self–other connection and the inherent reward of being a group member: "I helped, but we all did it together. Can you take a picture of me and my friends with this? I want to show my teacher."

Outcome Studies

To date, there have been three outcome studies published on the efficacy of the "LEGO® Club" social development approach. The first (LeGoff 2004) utilized a waiting-list designed to provide a pre-treatment comparison with which to compare participants, both male and female, who were involved in weekly small groups using the LEGO-Based Therapy approach. The participants (N = 47) were all diagnosed with an ASC condition—referred to in the *Diagnostic and Statistical Manual of Mental Disorders, Fourth Edition* (*DSM-IV*) as Pervasive Developmental Disorders (PDD; APA 2000)—and all had demonstrated difficulties with social interaction and communication with peers, social aloofness, as well as repetitive, persistent, or excessive interests and rigid adherence to non-functional rules or rituals. All were referred for intervention by either their respective school district special services staff or by their parents. The participants whose treatment was deferred by the waiting list were assessed and their social functioning was compared later with measures of social competence after they had been actively receiving treatment. Some participants were on the waiting list for three months (N = 26), and some were on the waiting list for six months (N = 21). All participants subsequently received at least six months of LEGO-Based Therapy.

The assessment of the participants during the waiting list phase was conducted at the initial referral, three months later, and then, if they were still on the waiting list, again after six months. Similarly, once the participant was active in a "LEGO® Club", they were assessed after three months of participation, and then after six months of participation. For each participant, measures of their frequency of self-initiated social contact with peers, duration of social interaction with peers during free-play, and the frequency and severity of repetitive or idiosyncratic behaviors were collected.

Statistical comparisons were made between pre-treatment and post-treatment levels on each of these three measures. There were no differences found on these measures at the initial assessment, that is, after the wait period and prior to starting treatment, but after only three months there was a significant improvement on all three measures. The frequency of self-initiated contact with peers during free play increased from pre-treatment levels by 69 percent after three months of LEGO-Based Therapy (from an average of 2.4 contacts per half hour of play to 4.1 contacts per half hour), and by 83 percent after six months (from 2.4 contacts to 4.4 contacts). Both of these were statistically significant, and clinically meaningful gains (i.e. not just statistically reliable, but subjectively noticeable to observers, parents, and teaching staff, even without statistical analysis). The duration of social interaction with peers during a one hour after-school free-play period also increased by statistically significant and meaningful lengths of time, from 21 minutes at baseline to 36.5 minutes after three months of treatment (74.0% increase), and from 19.7 minutes during the waiting list phase to 55.7 minutes after six months of treatment (182.6% increase). The third measure involved ratings of rigid, repetitive behaviors and idiosyncratic interests. On this measure, the participants improved by 13.5 percent after three months of treatment, and 28.1 percent after six months, and this was again both statistically significant and was considered to be a meaningful improvement.

In the second study (LeGoff and Sherman 2006), 60 "LEGO® Club" participants who were diagnosed with an ASC were compared over a longer period of time (three years), with a matched group of participants (N = 57) who were also diagnosed with PDDs and who were receiving comparable levels of intervention over the same period of time. The two groups were compared before and after treatment on a measure of social development, the Vineland Adaptive Behavior Scales, Socialization Domain (VABS-SD; Sparrow, Balla, and Cicchetti 1984), and autistic behaviors, the Gilliam Autism Rating Scale, Social Interaction sub-scale (GARS-SI; Gilliam 1995).

Although both groups showed significant improvement in ratings of social development and sustained these improvements over time, the LEGO-Based Therapy participants improved significantly more than the non-LEGO-Based Therapy participants. On the Vineland SD scale, the control group participants improved by 18.0 percent over a three-year period, while the LEGO-Based Therapy participants improved by 33.2 percent, which is a 15.2 percent gain over and above the improvement of similar participants receiving the same levels of intervention. This was a statistically significant difference. On the GARS-SI, which assesses repetitive, stereotyped behaviors and idiosyncratic interests (also used in the previous study), the comparison group improved by 20.9 percent, while the "LEGO Club" improved by 31.2 percent, which is a 10.3 percent difference between the groups in terms of long-term outcome, and, again, this was a statistically significant difference.

These two studies established that the LEGO®-Based Therapy method appeared to be having a meaningful and sustained impact on measures of social development for its participants, compared with both no treatment (waiting list) and other treatments. This improvement was clearly statistically significant and clinically meaningful within a fairly short period of time (three months), and was evident in a range of socially adaptive behaviors after a much longer time period (three years). Perhaps most importantly, the measures used included both direct observation of the participants in natural social settings without adult direction or support, and ratings of their social development in a broad sense.

Following the publication of these two initial outcome studies, a third, independent assessment of the LEGO-Based Therapy method was undertaken at Cambridge University's Autism Research Centre by our co-authors, Gómez de la Cuesta (née Owens) and Baron-Cohen, and their colleagues (Owens *et al.* 2008). In this study, 6–11-year-olds with autism or Asperger's Syndrome were randomly assigned to one of two groups—a "LEGO Club" social group, or a therapy group based on a widely used social communication therapy, the Social Use of Language Programme (SULP; Rinaldi 2004)—and attended once a week for 18 weeks. University students were trained by the researchers to follow the LEGO method and they provided group therapy to half of the participants, while the other half participated in the ongoing SULP programe. Comparisons on measures of social development were made at the beginning and end of the therapy programs. These groups were then compared with an age- and IQ-matched comparison group who received no intervention. The three studies described have also been discussed and elaborated upon in two subsequent publications (LeGoff *et al.* 2010, 2011).

Results showed improvements in social competence in both intervention groups compared with children who received no intervention. Children who received LEGO®-Based Therapy showed greater improvements in maladaptive behavior, autism-specific social difficulties, and duration of social interaction with peers. Children who receieved SULP improved more on measures of social communication. While this study had several methodological issues, it was an important independent study demonstrating improvements in social competence in children with ASC following LEGO-Based Therapy. Children and parents alike were very satisfied with the LEGO-Based Therapy intervention, and found the approach enjoyable, stress-free, and motivating.

This manual presents a comprehensive description of LEGO-Based Therapy and its components, such that professionals can set up their own therapy groups and researchers will be able to continue to evaluate its efficacy. The clinical approach used in LEGO-Based Therapy and outcome data from research are presented with three purposes in mind: first, to describe a therapy approach which appears to be interesting and engaging to the participants; second, to provide data on which to assess the therapeutic effectiveness of this approach in improving social competence in children with ASC and other conditions which affect social development; and third, to stimulate some thought about the nature of social competence, its component skills, and the effective strategies for enhancing it.

2

Implementing
LEGO®-Based Therapy

Overview

LEGO-Based Therapy is a collaborative play therapy in which children work together to build LEGO models. Instead of building LEGO sets by themselves, children work in pairs or teams of three or more. The task of LEGO building is divided into different but interdependent roles, such that interaction and both verbal and nonverbal communication are necessitated by participation in the activity. Key social experiences such as collaboration, joint attention, joint accomplishment, division of labor, sharing, turn-taking, eye-contact, gaze-following, verbal communication and nonverbal communication are emphasized and coached by the LEGO-Based Therapy staff, while members focus on the joint creative process. LEGO-Based Therapy can be used in both individual and group therapy modalities, during which natural opportunities are used to practice social communication, social support, social problem-solving, and conflict resolution skills.

Participants

LEGO-Based Therapy was initially developed for improving social competence in children with ASC. However, it may also be helpful for children with other social communication difficulties and anxiety conditions (especially social phobia), depression, or adjustment difficulties manifesting as depression or anxiety, though research has yet to evaluate the effectiveness of the approach with these difficulties. Experience suggests that LEGO®-Based Therapy may not be appropriate for mixed groups of children with very different clinical presentations: for example those with internalizing conditions such as ASC disorders (PDDs), anxiety disorders, and adjustment difficulties, and those with externalizing disorders such as ADHD or other aggressive, acting-out disorders (e.g. conduct disorder).

To date, LEGO-Based Therapy has been successfully implemented in outpatient clinical settings (i.e. outpatient mental health and neurodevelopmental clinics), public and private schools, and in rehabilitation facilities. Participation is always voluntary, not mandated, and alternative social activities are always offered. The typical participant is a child who has clearly identified difficulties with social engagement and social communication, and who has limited ability to access the usual extra-curricular peer-group activities (e.g. sports, playground participation, birthday parties, family gatherings).

Although non-affected, or typically developing, peers have been included in the past, there have been logistical issues, ranging from confidentiality to financial requirements. The inclusion of typical peers has also created problems when the peers are not well prepared and may verbalize criticism or dismay at the idiosyncrasies, atypical interests, and emotional fragility of the children with ASC or other conditions. Typical peers are often somewhat less motivated to attend the groups and, especially after a few weeks of attending, their attendance rate may become inconsistent. They have other social outlets, and are often more aware of the somewhat unusual social context: "Hey, Dr. Dan, why does a doctor have a 'LEGO® Club'?" Typical peers may not recognize the uniqueness of the group, and it is difficult for them to understand the confidentiality and other ethical issues involved: "Can I invite my neighbor and my cousin to come? They'd love this. We do a lot of building. Can we come on our own when these guys aren't here?" "My coach wants to know if we can have our soccer party here. That would be really cool."

There are extensive precedents for the use of trained peer mentors or peer models in classrooms to help with social development and improving classroom participation (Carter *et al.* 2005; Franca *et al.* 1990; Fuchs *et al.* 2002; Haring and Breen 1992; Kohler *et al.* 1997; Laushey and Heflin 2000; Whitaker *et al.* 1998), as well as learning and academic achievement (Cushing and Kennedy 1997; Dugan *et al.* 1995; Franca *et al.* 1990; Fuchs, Fuchs and Burish 2000; Greenwood, Carta, and Kamps 1990; Greenwood, Carta, and Hall 1988; Greenwood *et al.* 2001; Topping 1988). The focus of these strategies is most often a single child, however, and that child's adjustment to, and benefit from, a classroom setting. The goal of a "LEGO Club" includes a broader goal of overall social adjustment and social motivation, as well as creating a social milieu among peers with common difficulties and needs, in order to support and enhance identification with peers and motivation to participate in joint achievement and collaboration. Limitations in non-classroom settings (confidentiality, costs, available resources, and staffing), would make it difficult or impossible to implement strategies which emphasize extensive training of multiple peer tutors or mentors. Luckily, as the outcome research has demonstrated, social and behavioral outcomes using the current model are very encouraging, without the complications of including typical peers.

Implementation Staff

LEGO®-Based Therapy should be run by individuals who have a sound understanding of children with ASC and experience of working with children with developmental or social learning difficulties. Clinical psychologists, educational psychologists, speech and language pathologists, occupational therapists, mental health counselors, social workers, and special education teachers or educational specialists are all capable of running LEGO-Based Therapy groups. Alongside the main adult supervisor, additional support staff may be needed, depending on the size of the group, the age range, and the level of needs of the children. Typically, two adults are needed to help in a group of six children. The methods used in LEGO-Based Therapy are clearly outlined in this manual, and should be implemented by dedicated individuals who are experienced in working with children with ASC and related conditions.

The identification and diagnosis of potential participants should necessarily be undertaken by qualified mental health or neurodevelopmental specialists. The intake process used for the LEGO-Based Therapy groups is outlined below. As mentioned above, mixed groups which include children with both internalizing and externalizing symptomatologies has not been a successful strategy, and so some care with screening and intake procedures is warranted.

Creating a Positive and Effective Social Milieu (Group Environment)

It is especially important in a group setting where there is a high demand on staff resources and patience to be sure that all personnel have the appropriate level of training and experience to both know what to expect, and how to respond to atypical emotional responses, interpersonal style, and social responses. Labeling of otherwise inappropriate social behavior as "disrespectful," "rude," "inappropriate," or "impolite" is a waste of time, and creates a potentially pejorative and negative social environment. This is never helpful. Focusing on positive social communication is vital. Commenting on positive social interaction so that the other group members notice and can identify those actions which elicit positive attention and praise is much more effective. Saying what behavior you want, rather than telling participants what not to do, is very important. Even more effectively, prompting other group members to notice and comment on other group members' pro-social actions and helpfulness can elicit strong responses to peer praise, feelings of affiliation and acceptance, and group identification. Similarly, prompting peers to provide mild corrective responses to inappropriate actions in a social context such as a shake of the head, discouraging look, or a mild corrective comment are much more effective than repeated adult verbal prompts (i.e. nagging).

Acknowledgments of achievements by participants can be provided in both formal (see Chapter 6) and informal ways. Feedback to parents or caregivers at the end of each session should include mostly positive comments and notes about areas of strength and emerging skills. The Club should include an area with photos and other personal memorabilia of accomplishments to encourage joint achievements, as well as to build group identity and self-efficacy.

Basic Principles

The use of LEGO® as a means of facilitating social, behavioral, and cognitive development is an intervention approach which developed as a result of applying the following basic principles:

- LEGO®-Based Therapy is a skill-building approach. This assumes that problematic social interactions and deficits in the development of age-appropriate peer relationships result from underlying neurobiologically-based deficits in social development. As children improve in their social and adaptive functioning, self-regulation, and problem-solving, stereotypies and social deficits are replaced by more adaptive communicative gestures or self-regulatory gestures in all relevant settings.

- LEGO-Based Therapy capitalizes on the inherently rewarding and motivating aspects of constructive play and the system of LEGO materials themselves. The intervention thereby avoids the necessity for using secondary positive reinforcement in order to elicit and sustain appropriate participation in almost all cases. Secondarily, the motivational aspects of displaying mastery and skill acquisition in a social context, and the experience of social acceptance and mutual identification (i.e. bonding), continue to build, and eventually lead to social gains outside of the group.

- The core of the therapeutic intervention is a collaborative process, with inherent interdependence, creating a necessity for joint attention, shared goals, joint accomplishment, social communication, and mutual respect and valuation. Whenever possible, conflict situations, realistic frustrations, and limitations of the group structure and schedule, disappointments, disagreements, and so on are deflected by the staff to be resolved by the participants themselves. Staff are encouraged to support and coach or guide the process, but should not "join" the group, or solve their problems: they need to help each other, and work out solutions for themselves.

- While the focus for group participants will naturally be on the LEGO®-building projects, and the social, material, and natural hurdles involved, the focus of the therapy personnel should be on the social communication and collaboration of the participants. It is important to keep in mind that the LEGO projects themselves, while sometimes indicative of a good collaborative building process, are secondary to the ongoing communication and social process. The communication and social bonding occurs as a result of the joint focus on a common goal, the LEGO building, and is periodically reinforced by both the therapists' coaching of the communication and interpersonal relationship building and the identification of the joint nature of the goals and achievements ("Hey, look what you guys did together!").

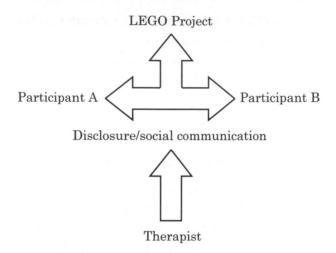

LEGO Project

Participant A

Participant B

Disclosure/social communication

Therapist

LEGO®-Based interventions emphasize social identity development. In creating a sense of common purpose and a shared interest in the LEGO play system, children who otherwise are typically socially isolated express feeling that they are part of a group of peers with whom they identify: for example, "These kids are from my planet—I belong here with them." Respecting and supporting the participants' idiosyncratic interests and atypical communication patterns at the outset creates a socially safe environment which encourages self–other identification: having achieved this important initial social identification, participants frequently express feeling more secure and confident about pursuing other relationships and more challenging social contexts.

- LEGO-Based Therapy has four progressive levels of achievement, with goals and challenges specific to each. Each level builds on the skills learned and mastery achieved in the previous levels, and is associated with therapeutic goals which both consolidate previous gains and introduce more advanced challenges. The process of achievement includes both overtly LEGO®-related building and creating skills (for example moving from basic LEGO tasks such as finding parts, to building sets, to doing freestyle creations) and social and communication skills, for example from pivotal skills such as self-monitoring and self-control, joint attention, listening to directions, following social and proscriptive rules, to higher-level skills such as being assertive without being aggressive, expressing interest in others' points of view and interests, calmly resolving conflicts with mutual benefit, expressing ideas effectively, providing positive feedback and accepting criticism and feedback from others, and trading favors. These levels are not rigidly applied, however, and participants may quickly move up or even skip a level, or require a review and reiteration during periodic regressions, or in order to review a skill deficiency. These levels are described in the next section.

3

LEGO®-Based Therapy
Modes of Intervention

Mode 1: Individual Therapy and Pivotal Skills

This is an optional mode designed primarily for use with many younger children, and those with cognitive and/or visual-motor deficits, who may need help with learning the basic skills of LEGO building. For this reason, the leader may wish to start with individual basic skill acquisition. Basic skills or "pivotal" skills (cf. Koegel and Koegel 1995; Leaf and McEachin 1999) necessary for higher-level activities include the following:

- Sitting in a chair at a table, without attempting to escape or wander off to explore the LEGO room or other rooms.

- Responding to verbal instructions and nonverbal prompts, including pointing and gaze direction, and imitating LEGO-building basic activities as demonstrated, with or without verbal prompting. These areas are typically addressed using a combination of adult feedback and social support for positive compliance (praise), self-monitoring and self-management exercises, and the use of trained peer models at times to enhance peer imitation and help establish norms and rule-following (Steege *et al.* 2007).

- With supervision, the participant should be able to consistently exhibit (on about four out of five attempts or opportunities) core building skills such as:

  ○ *sorting* similar LEGO® pieces by shape, color, and size, and placing similar pieces in grouped proximity

  ○ *finding* specific pieces either to match a similar LEGO piece or by looking at a picture or image of the piece

  ○ *identifying and labeling* LEGO pieces accurately by using verbal descriptors of color, shape, size, and function (e.g. brick, hinge, ladder, window, door, tool, roof shingle, floor plate)

  ○ *combining* pieces by their appropriate mechanism, from simple block-on-block connections, to more complex construction such as hinges, windows, doors, roof shingles, flags and standards, tools, animal and human mini-fig assembly, wheel and tire assemblies, gears and axles, etc.

  ○ *following simple visual instructions* with adult support, and adding the correct pieces in the correct order and placement in order to complete a simple LEGO set (about 20–40 pieces)

  ○ *following simple visual instructions* with a single peer, and adding the correct pieces in the correct order and placement in order to complete a simple LEGO set (about 20–40 pieces)

  ○ *inspecting* a completed set, mini-fig or sub-section of a LEGO set, and comparing it critically with the visual directions to find inconsistencies or mistakes, and subsequently either just identifying them or initiating correcting them.

- Not engaging in actions which appear aggressive or destructive in the therapy area or in the waiting or other sites, and not engaging in provocative, disruptive, or potentially aggressive or destructive actions in the presence of peers.

- Complying with basic compliance expectations, such as waiting appropriately, following a routine and structure for each session, respecting interpersonal space, and using appropriate physical contact.

- Cooperating with peers when introduced into a group setting.

- Being able to receptively and expressively communicate with peers effectively, either verbally or nonverbally.

Although many of these skills are prerequisites for group participation (e.g. sitting still, not engaging in aggression), others are skills that can be acquired in individual as well as group activities. The leader should communicate and collaborate with others involved, including parents, siblings, home-based therapists, teachers, speech-language therapists, and occupational therapists, in working on these goals. If possible, it is helpful to attend or host periodic team meetings to introduce other team members to the use of LEGO® as a medium, and to discuss goals, strategies, problems, and set-backs.

Children working on pivotal or Mode 1 skills can be included in groups with peers of similar levels, although these groups typically require 1:2 or 1:3 adult-to-participant ratios of supervision. In these groups, the group is led by a senior therapist, with additional support provided by qualified aides, students, or trainees, similar to levels of instruction and supervision necessary in a classroom setting. These groups should contain a balance of activities focused on three areas:

- building fine motor, visual-motor, and other basic building skills

- self-monitoring, self-control, and compliance with routines and adult direction

- social interaction and communication skills with peers.

Identifying Activities for Pivotal Skills

As mentioned above, a key element to the success of LEGO®-Based Therapy participation, especially early on, is the identification of preferred areas of interest or preoccupation. This can be determined by interview with the parents or educational staff, or by direct observation. Observation may be especially helpful when preferences are not clear or well established, or when a child has not had much exposure to LEGO materials.

An observational preference assessment can be implemented by allowing the child to freely explore a range of LEGO materials in a therapy room (this can be done during an initial interview), and noting the items with which they were engaged the longest. If they do not engage with the materials, or show any particular preferences, you may ask the parents about preferred play activities, sensory experiences, or color and texture preferences. Follow up these suggestions by presenting the child with a limited number of options (two or three at a time), within visual sight and arms' reach. Note which items are reached for consistently, especially if they go on to manipulate the items. Attempt to take the items from the child and place them just outside of their reach, but within sight. Note whether they request or otherwise indicate interest, by reaching, pointing, or vocalizing while looking at the item.

Typically, children will show a preference for at least one or two small display items, or for a particular container of freestyle pieces. Attempt to find at least two or three activities or items that consistently result in reaching or other signs of interest. Some children gravitate towards the LEGO® literature (catalogues and magazines). These can become preferred items on their own, or the child may indicate some items from the catalogue that are desired, either by nonverbal cues (staying on one page, pointing, etc.), or by verbal request. It may be useful to have parents or the Club acquire these items. It is also advised that duplicates of LEGO catalogues and magazines be available, as these tend to have a shorter life than the building materials, especially well-loved favorites.

Initiating Structured Activities
Introducing and assessing basic skills

Depending on the skill level and cooperativeness of the child, an individual therapist may wish to spend some time orienting a child to the LEGO-building process, and probing to assess their levels in the fine motor, self-management, and social communication domains. In order to allow for inclusion in a "LEGO Club," the child should have the basic building, self-control, and social rule-following skills in order not to be disruptive or require full-time 1:1 attention and supervision.

The first contact may include introduction of a small set which captures the child's previously assessed interests, and which is at a level which they can complete, with adult support and supervision if necessary. During this process, the therapist can informally assess the child's LEGO®-building skills. Allow some play-time with the completed model. Subsequently, the therapist should introduce some sorting, labeling, and identifying tasks, and then some examples of imitating a free style (e.g. "Look what I'm doing with my bricks. Can you do this? Make these bricks look like mine").

Small Set-building

It will be important to incorporate the child's interests or preferences in the initial sessions. If the child has shown a consistent interest in a small set or theme (e.g. Creator®, Sponge Bob®, Harry Potter®, Star Wars®, Ninjago®, Chima®), the set or sets can become the focus of initial sessions, by having the child construct the set from disassembled parts, using the directions, with adult support. The instructions may need to be modified, including enlarging them, laminating them, or by creating more detailed directions with additional sub-steps (this is difficult and time-consuming, and should be necessary only with severely delayed children). It is often helpful to have duplicates of favorite small sets so that the finished set can be used as reward for initiating set construction, or for doing pre-construction activities, for example sitting at the table, putting pieces into the tray, sorting the pieces, looking at the instructions.

If the child has chosen a small set that is beyond their building skills at the initial stage, and will not accept a smaller set, early instruction may begin with a partially completed set, with only the final few steps left unassembled. This can be highly motivating, and leads to early mastery experiences which are inherently rewarding.

Appropriate sitting and compliance with the task should be rewarded with access to the preferred set item. As the child is able to show consistent compliance for access to the completed set, the set can be progressively disassembled, with parts of the set used provided as reinforcement. Consistent with reinforcement principles of discrete trial instruction (cf. Leaf and McEachin 1999), the duration of sitting, and number of compliant responses necessary for receiving an additional part or piece of the set, can be increased over time. Keep in mind that the set may eventually lose interest for the child, and other sets may be substituted. Keeping track of items with which the child initiates play when they first enter the LEGO® room can help with keeping a set of desired items, which can be rotated as needed.

Pre-Building Skills

In order to prepare a child for collaborative building in groups, they need to develop basic motor and cognitive skills, including piece sorting, piece assembly, matching, and imitating. This can be done with freestyle pieces easily, and children can be rewarded for completing the activities with access to a preferred set or pieces of the set. As mentioned above, activities should include:

- sorting by color, shape, and size (e.g. "Put the red ones in here, the blue ones here")

- matching three-dimensional pieces (i.e. "Find another one like this")

- matching two-dimensional images (from instructions) with actual pieces ("We need one like this, look in the picture")

- piece assembly (i.e. "Put this one on top, press hard")

- imitation (i.e. "Can you make yours look like mine?")

- turn-taking (i.e. "Ok, you do the next one")

- simple collaborative building (i.e. "What should we build? What next? Show me").

Building Skills

Independent set-building can be initiated once the child shows independent abilities to identify pieces, sort and select pieces based on the instructions, and basic imitation. Medium-level sets (50–150 pieces) can be introduced. The LEGO® age guidelines provided on sets can be very useful in determining the next level for a given child. Parents should be encouraged to attempt sets at home that are at the next level of difficulty above the one most recently mastered. Often, at this level, the child may need some adult prompting and help, especially with parts that are more difficult to assemble (e.g. wheels, smaller parts), or finding pieces that fall on the floor or onto furniture from the table. Once they are able to consistently collaborate with an adult and stay focused on task appropriately, without having to use external reinforcement at each step (i.e. rewards can be delayed to final completion), the child is ready for collaborative building with a peer.

Mode 2: Collaborative Building with One Peer

Mode 2 activities involve collaborative building with one peer, and often require close adult supervision. It is often helpful, especially initially, to have a more advanced peer-mentor (or a typically developing peer if utilized) as a Helper (Pierce and Schreibman 1997). In this regard, we have often found it useful to match a child who is working on pro-social and helping skills with a learner. Although peer mentoring continues at all levels of the "LEGO® Clubs", at times such as this it is more explicitly the focus of the intervention.

Collaborative Set-Building

With pairs, it is often helpful to start off with sets that are within reach of the child who is being helped. As the pair demonstrates reciprocal building (e.g. they are able to complete a small set independently, with minimal adult intervention), the level of complexity of sets can be increased. The helping child may need to be given additional support and rewards for being patient and supportive at this stage, with access to preferred sets or magazines, for example, or by earning new sets or desired pieces. Typically, Helpers have difficulty allowing the less-skilled Builder to fully participate, and will tend to take over the task completely. For this reason, the adult should strictly regulate the activity by assigning specific tasks as follows:

- The child just starting Mode 2 will be the Parts Supplier. Their job is to find the correct LEGO pieces and give them to the child who they are working with.

- The more advanced member of the pair will be the Builder. Their job is to put the pieces together according to the instructions. (Care should be taken not to assign the role of Parts Supplier to a participant who is already capable of building.)

- The Parts Supplier should be encouraged and prompted primarily by the Builder, not the adult supervisor. For example, the Builder should prompt the Parts Supplier when they have finished one step and need the next piece.

The Builder should be instructed to follow a hierarchy of requests or prompts. First, the Builder will ask for specific parts needed to complete the set by verbally describing the pieces (e.g. "Please can I have a black two by two brick?"). Second, if the Parts Supplier gives the wrong piece or doesn't respond, the Builder should point to the item in the instructions, again giving the verbal label. Finally, if the Parts Supplier has not yet given the correct piece, the Builder should point to the actual piece, and again verbally label it. The Builder should not take pieces from the Parts Supplier, or take the Parts Supplier's hand to guide a response. Only when there is a clear failure of verbal and nonverbal requests should the adult give direct assistance by pointing or hand-over-hand prompting. The adult should also repeat the verbal prompt, and, if necessary, place the piece in the Parts Supplier's hand, and then prompt him or her to give the piece to the Builder.

This process of collaborative building with a peer is at the core of the LEGO®-Based Therapy process, and should be learned and perfected as a central skill-building strategy. All higher-level LEGO-Based Therapy activities are dependent on mastery of this initial collaborative task.

Once a Parts Supplier has shown some mastery of this task, that is, the child spontaneously gives parts and needs fewer nonverbal prompts, then turn-taking should be introduced. In this situation, the set is either divided according to number of steps (e.g. one child is Builder for the first 20 of 40 steps and the second child is Builder for the final 20 steps), or by functional design characteristics of the set (e.g. building different parts, or sections of a set). On larger sets, with pairs collaborating, it may be necessary to switch more than once during the completion (e.g. switching every ten steps). Alternatively, turn-taking can be determined by time, for example swap roles every five or ten minutes.

Collaborative Freestyle Building

Once a child is able to sustain consistent turn-taking and collaboration with a peer on set-building, they can be introduced to paired freestyle building. Freestyle building is designing and building your own creations from non-set-specific LEGO® pieces, rather than following printed instructions to build a particular model. The adult can help steer the pair towards possible projects which have good potential for success.

Freestyle building involves an increased demand for communication, sharing of ideas, and joint attention collaboration. The pair should initially be led by the more advanced child. Their role is now the Engineer, and they are in charge of designing the freestyle creation. The less skilled child, who is working at Mode 2, combines the roles of Parts Supplier and Builder.

The emphasis in freestyle building should be on both effective communication and collaboration. Problem-solving, compromise, and turn-taking may need to be encouraged, modeled, and supported by the adult. If there is little success initially (e.g. the Engineer just takes over and the Builder winds up watching or making suggestions which are ignored) the adult should take a more active role. In this situation, the adult should join in a subservient role (Parts Supplier or Assistant Builder), not as Engineer.

Once the pair has demonstrated some proficiency at independently designing and completing freestyle creations, the less experienced child is ready to take over the role of Engineer. Again, the adult may need to be more involved initially, and, again, should assist rather than direct the project. Typically, at this stage, the LEGO® Helper will be given a symbolic diploma, recognizing their achievement and new status as LEGO Builder, and is eligible for inclusion in a larger group setting with age/developmental peers.

Mode 3: Collaborative Building with Two Peers
Collaborative Set-Building

Group set-building within "LEGO Clubs" usually involves small sub-groups. With some of the larger projects undertaken by the older groups, there are often five or six participants working on a project, but with younger groups (age 12 and under) there are usually no more than three participants working on a given project. In the dyads and triads, the members are assigned different building tasks.

The Engineer describes which parts are required and where to put them according to the instructions. Bricks can be described according to their color, shape, and size. For example:

- Blue, 1 x 1 brick

- Red, 1 x 2 brick

- Yellow, 2 x 2 brick

- Black, corner brick

- Yellow light

- White post

LEGO® terminology, however, evolves differently in different groups. A good place to look to find appropriate names for bricks that are quite complicated in shape is the

LEGO Factory website, on the "Pick a Brick" pages (http://shop.lego.com/en-US/Pick-A-Brick-ByTheme). Here you will also find images of the bricks listed above.

Once the Engineer has described the bricks, the Parts Supplier searches through the bricks to find the piece that the Engineer has specified and passes the pieces one at a time to the Builder. Typically, all the bricks are on shallow plastic trays (typical of cafeterias) rather than out on a table so that pieces are less likely to fall onto the floor and get lost or damaged.

The Parts Supplier may have additional tasks during building, such as cleaning parts for re-assembly for restoration projects, or sorting parts for pre-assembly on larger projects. The Parts Supplier may also be assigned some pre-assembly when there are a large number of simple units needed (e.g. pre-assembling wheels, axles, and tires). The Builder is given the pieces by the Parts Supplier and constructs the LEGO set according to the pictographic instructions accompanied by verbal directions from the Engineer.

The participants then take it in turns at each of the different roles (e.g. switching at a third of the way through a set of instructions—for a set with 90 steps, the participants would switch roles at step 30 and again at step 60). Here is a useful opportunity to practice turn-taking in a fair way. It is useful to ask the participants to generate fair strategies to decide who gets to be Builder first (usually everyone wants this job). If they cannot come up with their own idea, then you can prompt them to do "eenie meenie miny moe" or "scissors, paper, stone" or another appropriate and fair strategy. This is usually not a problem if participants are reminded that they will each share an equal number of steps in each role during the completion of the set.

With most groups of five or more participants, there should be at least two adults in the LEGO® room to facilitate and supervise. As noted above with single-peer collaborations, it is important not to take a leading role in the set-building, and defer most conflicts or problems to the members themselves. Participants often seek out the adults for help, but should be redirected to their peers in the group as appropriate resources. In some situations (e.g. a critical missing LEGO® piece), the entire group may be solicited to provide help. "Search parties" are common during groups in which larger projects are underway. It is very easy to identify a missing piece by set and part number. If participants frequently keep track of pieces, it is possible to avoid the "all but one" set turning into an "almost none" set.

In younger groups (aged eight and under) there are more dyads than triads, and there is a need for closer adult supervision. Off-task distractibility and wandering is more frequent, and should be tolerated, as long as the participants can return to the group, with peer-mediated prompting, when necessary: "Hey, I still need your help!" Set-building can be very technical and demands considerable attention and close interpersonal contact. Younger group members can rarely tolerate this for more than about 20 minutes at a time. Although some older group members can spend a full hour or 90 minutes building sets, the younger ones will need to have breaks during which they can play with the sets or do some relaxed freestyle building.

Collaborative Freestyle Building

Group freestyle building is the most common "LEGO Club" activity. Groups that start with set-building usually become freestyle groups eventually. In a larger group, it is difficult to maintain close supervision during freestyle building. There is a greater need for movement around the materials, and typically there is more noise and off-task behavior as well.

When one participant has an idea for a freestyle design, he or she is encouraged to share the idea with the group, and other group members are recruited to help. This typically results in two or three small groups working with the Engineer who had the idea, and two Builders/Parts Suppliers, who assist. The duration of interaction during freestyle building tends to be shorter, as diverging interests draw group members in different directions. Participants are often cued or prompted to recruit Helpers, especially when they seek advice or assistance from the adults. For example:

> Phillip: "Hey Dr. Dan, I need another black wheel like this one."

> Dr. Dan: "I know we have one somewhere, not sure where. Who's helping you?"

> Phillip: "No one. I'm building this by myself."

> Dr. Dan: "Can't do that Phil, buddy. You'll need help. Find a Helper."

> Phillip: "Hey who wants to help me find this wheel? Curt? Help me."

Freestyle building in small groups can often take the form of competitions. For example, two triads may be challenged to create the best space ship, monster truck, fire station. The group members and the group leaders later judge the results—they should be allowed to come up with their own judging criteria without much adult interference. Or there may be some objective assessment procedure, such as a race, completion of a stunt or trick, or a "drop test" (LEGO® creations are tested for engineering quality by being dropped from a certain height—the creation that loses the fewest pieces wins).

Mode 4: Social Communication—Individual Therapy

Although some participants attend only paired and/or group sessions, many also attend individual therapy, both initially to build pivotal skills but also later to address specific behavioral or communication challenges. This is often a good opportunity to learn and rehearse communication strategies which can then be practiced with peers in the group sessions. Straightforward skills such as appropriate greetings (learning other participants' names using photos, nonverbal communication such as a high-five in place of a handshake, making and sustaining eye contact) can be practiced in individual sessions. Individual sessions are also often used to raise awareness about potentially stigmatizing stereotypies, excessive preoccupations, or vocal or motor tics and/or mannerisms which may be affecting the peer-group dynamics.

Focal issues such as these may be addressed in individual sessions, or with parents, or even the whole family, since the potentially disruptive or stigmatizing issue is often also a problem at home as well as in the group sessions. Often, just raising awareness of the problem produces almost immediate results. Some more entrenched problems may be represented by, for example, a tic disorder or Tourette's Syndrome, trichotillomania (TTM), habit disorder, Jacksonian partial motor seizure, or stereotyped movement disorder. These issues should be addressed through the use of appropriate clinical interventions (e.g. habit reversal protocol, self-monitoring and self-management protocol, and/or pharmacotherapy). Similarly, co-morbid obsessive-compulsive rituals and routines may occur—these are typically distinguished from excessive interests or stereotyped movements by being ego-dystonic, that is, they are troublesome or stressful to the participant, though this is not always the case (Christophersen and Mortweet 2001).

Periodically, participants will be adversely affected by negative or stressful life events (e.g. family issues, family move or change of school, loss of a parent or other relative, loss of a pet), and anxiety and mood/irritability may be apparent, with diminished sociability and coping. Again, these issues can be introduced and discussed among trusted peers, but should also be addressed outside of the group through individual and/or family therapy.

Other more complex social communication skills can also be worked on, including active listening and expressing empathy, social problem-solving and conflict resolution, and assertiveness for example. For these skills, it is important to utilize examples and situations which occurred in the group context, so that there are no hypothetical situations, which tend not to be effective in eliciting the appropriate coping strategies in natural settings. During individual sessions, participants are asked to review events that occurred during groups, sometimes with videotaped evidence to enhance recall and provide cues for self-monitoring and perspective taking. Following this, the participant is encouraged to role-play alternative responses or to practice skills. For example:

Dr. Dan: "Tony, remember when Burt came to group last week? He was late."

Tony: "Yeah, he was late."

Dr. Dan: "What was he doing when he came in?"

Tony: "He was being late."

Dr. Dan: "Yes, but what else?"

Tony: [Laughing] "He was crying."

Dr. Dan: "Right, he was upset about being late. It bothered him. What did you do when you saw him?"

Tony: "I teased him… Oh, I said 'Cry baby, did you poop your diaper?'"

Dr. Dan: "Yeah. Then what happened?"

Tony: "Burt threw the train, and broke it. He ran out there, and he was knocking things in the waiting room!"

Dr. Dan: "Do you think you made him more upset?"

Tony: "Yeah, I think so. I shouldn't have teased him."

Dr. Dan: "Ok. So what could you have said to him instead of teasing?"

Tony: "I should have said 'it's ok, don't worry.'"

Dr. Dan: "How about this, I'll pretend to be Burt, and you practice saying something that will help me feel better."

Potentially stigmatizing repetitive actions, such as thumb-sucking, hair-twirling, nose-picking, hand-flapping, repetitive speech mannerisms or vocalizations, can be addressed in individual therapy, and then prompted or reminded with an agreed-upon cue or gesture during subsequent group sessions. This cueing or prompting of corrective actions is also often usefully shared with peers, who might prompt an appropriate alternative gesture (e.g. thumb under chin, forefinger at mouth, rather than thumb in mouth; fists pumped in excitement as opposed to hand-flapping). Again, these should be arranged and implemented only by qualified therapy staff.

4

LEGO®-Based Therapy
Group Sessions

Group sessions are typically scheduled once per week, for between 75 and 90 minutes. The first and last 10–15 minutes involve transitioning in and out of the session to the waiting area, and typically include parent contact and feedback. During these times, it is often important to gather information from parents regarding their perceptions of progress, or lack of progress, as well as any significant life events (positive—birthdays, new pets, new siblings, achievements at school or socially; or negative—losses, frustrations, disappointments). Upcoming absences including family trips, holidays, medical appointments, and so on should be shared by parents so that staff can plan for changes in group sizes, dynamics, and any other issues.

Group sessions, out of necessity, tend to be more structured and uniform than individual sessions. In general, the format in a group session moves from a higher degree of structure and control by the therapists, to more self-directed and less structured activity towards the end. The first part of the session sets the tone for the rest of the time so it is important to have a strong presence and a clear agenda at the outset. Participants are often excited and easily distracted and impulsive at the start of "LEGO Club" sessions. The process of greeting members, and talking briefly with their parents or caregivers, can be a difficult and even chaotic transition. There should be a clear set of options, or an established procedure in order to get the group into the therapy room or area as quickly as possible, and then engaged in a group-focused semi-structured activity or discussion.

Initial Greeting and Waiting Room Transition

Participants may or may not acknowledge other group members in the waiting room with age-appropriate greetings and eye contact, for example. This can be modeled by the staff, and responses to greetings by more reclusive, socially anxious members can be praised. Some prompting of peers to initiate peer greetings, and even greetings and exchanges with other group members' parents, is a good opportunity for practicing appropriate social greetings with adults.

Therapists unfamiliar with current trends in verbal and nonverbal greetings among different age groups should try to observe some typical age peers engaged in greetings, for example at school, a sporting event, or other social gathering. Gender, age, and sociocultural differences should be taken into account. Typically developing children and adolescents do not shake hands, or greet each other by name, unless calling out to get someone's attention. Physical contact is limited unless among close male friends (mock aggression), and eye contact in group settings is usually fleeting and brief, except among close female friends. Female peers will often notice and comment about hair and clothing choices, but typical boys do not, unless a clothing item was intended to elicit comments (e.g. a flashy pair of shoes, or a provocative t-shirt or hat).

There is often a clothing issue: either the members take off clothing (jackets, sweaters, hats, etc.) and/or shoes (and socks), and throw them down in the LEGO® room somewhere, or they may go to the work areas still wearing heavy outdoor clothing, and even backpacks, or personal music devices. In any case, this is a busy coaching time, for the interpersonal greeting, name-learning, and the clothing issues. Again, familiarity with age, gender, and cultural norms is a must.

Leaving behind electronic devices (music, games, video, phones, etc.), is often a difficult issue, and should be made a hard-and-fast rule at the outset. Although the participants will often interact and communicate about electronic media equipment and games in the waiting area, they should not bring these with them into the therapy area as they are distracting and inevitably lead to conflicts between group members or with staff. If group members manage to sneak in games or other electronic media devices, simply remind them of the rule, and ask them to take the item back to the waiting room, or simply set it aside in the therapy room, with the clear indication that they can have it back after the group session is over.

Food items are a similar issue. Given the limitations in terms of scheduling therapy sessions which are held outside of school hours, snacking or meal time may overlap with "LEGO® Club." We have not found it necessary to restrict food or eating in the waiting area, but have asked participants and their families to clean up after themselves, and not bring food or snacks into the LEGO-Based Therapy area. Parental support on this issue can be helpful.

Planning

Following the transition from the waiting room, the group typically convenes in the therapy room, and if they do not do so spontaneously, the therapy staff should continue to model and initiate greetings and social updates, model greeting of each other, and social banter, and then prompt or cue leading group members to do likewise: "Jay. How you doing? Anything new with you this week? How're the Phillies doing? Why don't you check in with your buddy Phil?" This becomes a fairly spontaneous and natural process after a few weeks, and little prompting is typically necessary; however, therapists are encouraged to continue to participate in socially appropriate greetings, typical of most educational and work settings. Allowing free-play at the beginning of a session, as opposed to the end, makes it much more difficult to divert the group members back to focusing on the group activity, as opposed to solo pursuits.

The planning discussions regarding the goals for the remainder of the session—that is, choosing a LEGO® project—can be a quick process, or sometimes can take up the rest of the session. With younger participants, the therapists may need to take more of a lead in helping them decide on a realistic and specific project. Older participants, especially adolescents, may already arrive with agreed-upon plans (worked out during the week over the internet, and printed out in bullet format).

There is often a strong pressure on participants to convince other group members to join them in their proposed or ongoing project, but there are often quick alliances and agreements for reciprocal exchanges, as the time for the group is dwindling during any debating. Therapists should not interrupt or try to resolve a stalled group unilaterally. Prompting and cueing participants to reciprocate or trade off favors can be helpful, but the process of discussion and argument is very appropriate and useful—grist for the mill.

Role and Task Assignment

Once there is a consensus regarding a project in general, the group members are then prompted to take roles, or components of the overall project, and responsibilities are assigned by the project leaders or Engineer(s). Encourage the group to engage in discussion with each other, either as a whole group or in sub-groups, on what needs to be done in order to meet their activity goals for the day, including dividing up the time among tasks. This is an especially important feature of sharing the available time among disparate points of view. Help the group members to work out compromise solutions, and keep track of favors given and owed. If participants are resistant to taking on an assigned role, the leader(s) should be prompted to negotiate with the participant regarding their preferences for participation. This can get quite involved and may require some prompting and support for the group leader to be assertive, convincing, and persuasive. Calling up owed favors, or asking for help with the promise of an owed favor at the next session, is often a good strategy.

Once the overall project is identified, the roles and responsibilities are usually fairly straightforward, or may be determined by doing an impromptu task analysis. Prompting the group leader(s) to review the tasks necessary to complete the project can get this rolling: "Charles, you'll be the Engineer on this project, how many Builders do you think we'll need? Ok, and how many Parts Suppliers? Who do you think would be good for this? You better talk to them."

Group-Based Semi-Structured Activities

This is typically the core of the group session, and during which the group members are actively engaged in an activity. During this time, the therapists may not need to be very active with members, or less so, depending on the skills and developmental level of the group. It also depends on the novelty of the task. For newer, less familiar tasks, there is a need for much more input from the therapists. Younger group members or inexperienced Builders also tend to require more input. If the group activity is chosen appropriately, the therapist should be able to focus almost entirely on the social and communication coaching, and leave the project management to the Engineer(s).

It is best to try to limit the group to an achievable number and complexity of tasks at the beginning. This can take some experience in order to know how long a given building task may take. For set-building (i.e. completing a boxed LEGO® set, with instructions), a rule-of-thumb formula for gauging time requirements is:

$$\frac{\text{Number of LEGO pieces involved}}{\text{Developmental age of group members (years)}} = \text{Time (minutes)}$$

For example, a group of children with the building skills of average ten-year-olds can put together a LEGO set with 600 pieces in 60 minutes. Keep in mind that that is an uninterrupted and intensive 60 minutes. Alternatively, a group of children with developmental age of four years would accomplish the same task in about 150 minutes.

During the actively engaged building time, the therapists should also be very active, circling the LEGO® room, observing and listening to the interaction. Violations of basic interaction rules, or being socially inappropriate— for example, not looking at someone when speaking, repeating phrases, changing the subject spontaneously and tangentially, leaving the work area without a reason, violating interpersonal space—can be addressed with gentle, whispered reminders or, even better, by prompting other group members to cue them back to task or to become aware of an inappropriate or potentially stigmatizing pattern: "Jim, why don't you ask Phil who he's talking to... Charlie, do you think it's ok that Lisa talks to you without looking at you? No? Why don't you ask her to look at you next time... Is he doing your job, Peter? Tell him that's your job. You're not in his pile, tell him to do his own work, and you'll do yours."

Less Structured, Creative Time

Following the main structured activity, there is often some time remaining, and this is a good time to allow a relaxation of structure and allow the members to pursue their own interests and projects. As much as possible, during this time, it is useful to try to link members up in pairs to work on joint projects, or link together members who may be engaging in play activities with similar themes.

During sessions, the participants are prompted unobtrusively to engage in a rehearsed communication skill. Depending on the results, we may do some practice in the group, with other participants helping and, at times, role-playing. As much as possible, these scenarios should be led by the more senior group members, and they should be encouraged to provide supportive corrective feedback and suggestions to their peers—a quick review with group members, with a prompt such as, "So, okay, we got through that. What did we all learn about how to handle that situation, Burt?"

Participant role-playing occurs more in older groups, especially during the first part of the session, which in 12-years-and-older groups is dedicated to social communication skills during a 15-minute period called "check-in." During "check-in" the members are restricted from LEGO® projects for the first 15 or 20 minutes, and are instructed to present to the group any significant or emotional event that occurred in the past week since the last group session.

Participants are asked to listen, and not interrupt the presenter, and each takes a turn, giving a brief description of the event (about two or three minutes). When the participant has finished, the other group members are encouraged to respond. Expressions of empathy and support are encouraged and praised, while problem-solving suggestions are supported, but not as enthusiastically. Group members who express hostility, or who offer inappropriate suggestions, are either ignored, or other group members are asked to comment on the suggestion. Role reversal during role-play of real scenarios is sometimes used to enhance empathy, both receptive (understanding another's emotions and experience) and expressively (responding in a way that helps the other feel heard and understood).

Clean-Up Time

Start giving clean-up time warnings about five to ten minutes ahead of time, depending on how involved and complex the ongoing projects are, and the extent of mess in the LEGO® room. Give at least two or three warnings before announcing clean-up time. Following the first warning, make sure no new projects are started, and no new play themes or LEGO sets are taken down from the shelf: "Don't start anything new, it's almost clean-up time, you have three minutes to finish up what you're doing." Announce clean-up time at roughly 15 minutes prior to the group ending—don't be flexible about this, or the group leader will spend an inordinate amount of time ordering and cleaning the materials. Be sure to indicate that all materials have to be put back where they came from, and all members should help each other put materials back, and not just put back the ones they were personally using.

This is a good team-building exercise. Remind them that any pieces left on the floor will go into the vacuum cleaner. We have routinely offered "LEGO® Points" to younger members for gathering up stray LEGO.

Farewell and Parent Review

Once the LEGO room is put back in order and everything is off the floor, cue group members to give age-appropriate farewells, including use of members' names. While group members are rotating through their farewells, I usually head out to the waiting room to give a brief feedback to parents about the group session, progress, problems, concerns, and so on. There is inevitably a second set of farewells in the waiting room, and often a continuation of this process out the door. At times, parents may be late in getting their child following a group. This elicits a wide range of reactions from the members, few of which are positive. A couple of times parents have neglected to return to pick up their child following a group. It is a good idea to remind parents ahead of time that this is not acceptable, and that they need to be on time to get their child after the group. Of course, this is not a problem for school-based or other groups in which parent transportation is not an issue.

Planning and Evaluating the Sessions

It is important to plan and evaluate each group session in order for targets to be assessed and progress to be made. An example planning and evaluation sheet is given in Appendix C.

5

Effective and Ineffective Strategies in LEGO®-Based Therapy

Various procedures and group make-ups have been tried in the development of LEGO-Based Therapy. Some have been successful, some less so. Effective and ineffective strategies are outlined in Table 5.1.

Table 5.1 Effective and ineffective strategies in LEGO-Based Therapy

Effective Strategies	Ineffective Strategies
Siblings attending groups as Helpers (though they must be prepared and attend regularly).	Including siblings who are disruptive or pursue their own goals and agenda and do not assist with group activities.
Including therapeutic aides, graduate students, or other trained helpers (but not parents).	Including parents or allowing parents or other family members to attend, or using untrained and inexperienced helpers or guests, can cause a number of problems. Aside from confidentiality issues, untrained guests or observers are often disruptive and negatively affect the group dynamics. Allowing parents to sit in to observe the group was a mistake in almost all cases—the children acted very differently with a parent in the LEGO room.

cont.

Table 5.1 Effective and ineffective strategies in LEGO-Based Therapy *continued*

Effective Strategies	Ineffective Strategies
Allowing group members free-play time to be creative and participate in role-based fantasy play with the figures and sets, rather than just building, leads to increased spontaneous interaction among group members.	Being overly structured and sticking to a therapist-led agenda at all times. This inhibits the "Club" feeling, decreases the inherently positive reinforcement and motivation of participation, and limits the naturalistic activity, interaction and communication among group members. During free-time, the therapists should continue to shadow and coach social and communication opportunities.
Encouraging female group members to join—this is especially helpful in older groups in which adolescent developmental issues are discussed.	Although the numbers are typically skewed towards males, female group members are invariably a positive addition. In particular, the creative and collaborative efforts of the group often improve.
Allowing group members to join each other and family members for meals or snacks prior to groups, either at an agreed-upon location, home or in the waiting room, especially during special occasions e.g. Christmas, birthdays, bar-mitzvahs etc.	Providing or allowing food or snacks in the LEGO® room during groups was a disaster. LEGO bricks are hard to clean, and even "safe" snacks (e.g. hard candy, gum) can turn into an irretrievable mess in the right hands.

Having a 10–15 minute "check-in" time in which members are asked to give a verbal account of personal experiences or to share views.	Allowing members to rush into the group and start in with their projects from the previous week, or just initiate freestyle building or exploring the LEGO room. Instead, groups should be structured and start with a group focus, and then shift to less structured and individualized pursuits after the main group activity is complete.
Children with a range of developmental and behavioral issues can be included, but those whose primary issues (behaviorally and socially) are impulsive, should be pre-screened and referred to other modes of intervention. These members can be re-screened at a later date, once the behavioral issues have been addressed to determine if underlying social development issues persist and still need to be remediated.	Including children with behavior conditions, such as Attention deficit hyperactivity disorder (ADHD), Oppositional defiant disorder (ODD), or other externalizing conditions, who also have social skill problems, is not productive. These group members are often disruptive and interfere with the group identification process for many other group members
Group members making joint decisions about issues that affect the group, for example, choosing new LEGO®, activities for the day, and promotions of members.	Group discussions and joint decision-making are core features of this method. Loud, dominant members should be discouraged from making unilateral decisions, and input from all members should be sought for any decision that affects others. Also avoid having group leaders resolve conflicts and make decisions for the group: let them work it out.

cont.

Table 5.1 Effective and ineffective strategies in LEGO-Based Therapy *continued*

Effective Strategies	Ineffective Strategies
Assigning mentors for newer group members, and encouraging pro-social helping and teaching.	New group members who are anxious or inhibited, and allowed to "take a back seat" to more assertive members, often do not come back.
Encouraging families to develop a support and activity network outside of LEGO-Based Therapy.	Restricting group member and family contact to the group restricts development of more natural and generalized social contact. This is necessary in some therapeutic groups, but with some guidance and input, this can be a very helpful component of the therapy.
Including children with anxiety conditions, especially social phobia, depression, or adjustment difficulties, manifesting as depression or anxiety, in the group. Many of them continue to attend as Helpers log after their presenting problems are resolved.	Children whose social problems arise from other co-morbid internalizing conditions suffer just as much from social development issues, and benefit just as much, often more quickly, compared with ASC clients. Over-selection of groups to provide better group cohesion and group identification is a potential benefit, but at the cost of generalization of improvements, and the loss of group members who may be good role models for social communication and social reasoning.

6

Behavior Management and Rewards

"LEGO® Club" Rules

Parents, as well as teachers and other therapists who are not familiar with this treatment approach, often ask about discipline or behavior control procedures. It turns out that these problems are quite rare when using this approach, especially when the participants are highly motivated and have been properly prepared during the initial interview and first few group sessions.

A key to LEGO-Based Therapy is establishing self-regulation, and using peer-mediated corrective feedback. These skills are aided by the use of posted rules, the "LEGO Club" Rules. During the initial interview, potential participants are told, "If you want to come to the 'LEGO Club,' you have to be able to follow the rules." For nonverbal or pre-verbal children, this message is usually conveyed by correcting their behavior during individual therapy sessions. Children without verbal communication skills are not included in groups until they are proficient at the required skill set, which includes behavioral compliance. The LEGO Rules were developed by the original participants in the first LEGO-Based social skills groups, and reflect the consensus regarding a necessary and sufficient set of rules for peer-mediated regulation of the group process:

"LEGO® Club" Rules:

- If you break it, you have to fix it.

- If you can't fix it, ask for help.

- If someone else is using it, don't take it, ask first.

- No yelling. Use indoor voices.

- No climbing or jumping on furniture.

- No teasing, name-calling or bullying.

- No hitting or wrestling—keep hands and feet to yourself.

- Clean up—put things back where they belong.

These rules are printed in large type so they can be easily read, and are posted on the poster board in the LEGO room so they can be referred to whenever necessary. Whenever a new member is introduced to a group, one or more of the group members are asked to review the rules with the new member, and we often then have a group discussion about how each of the members has occasionally needed to be corrected about a rule violation.

An important aspect of having the rules is implementing them consistently, and without negativity. The therapist should typically not offer direct feedback regarding rule violations. Instead, whenever possible, the therapist(s) will request the other participants in the group to remind each other about the rules. Using indirect and ambiguous terms enhances the participants' abilities to identify when someone else is breaking a rule, as well as for themselves. For example, when a child climbs onto a chair to retrieve something from a high shelf:

Dr. Dan: "Hey guys, is someone in here breaking a rule?"

David: "Uh, yeah, Peter is hogging the big truck wheels."

Dr. Dan: "Yeah...you have to talk to him about that. Anything else?"

Peter: "Yes! Sam is climbing on furniture. Get down Sam, that's rule number 5."

Dr. Dan: "Good point, Peter. Sam?"

Sam: "Sorry, Dr. Dan, I just wanted to get R2D2 for my X-wing."

Dr. Dan: "Well, what should you do?"

Sam: "I couldn't reach it without getting up..."

Dr. Dan: "'LEGO® Club', what should Sam do?"

Group (together): "He should ask for help!"

LEGO Points

A formal "LEGO Points" system can be used, in which points are awarded for pro-social and LEGO-related achievements (e.g. complying with rules, building models with another child). These points can be collected and traded in for LEGO prizes (small sets, LEGO people, etc.). Prizes can be useful initially, but after a while points tend to become inherently valuable, and not associated with any tangible reward. Instead, children seek the social approval of earning points. For this reason, points are an option in implementing LEGO-Based Therapy. The use of LEGO Points is typically reserved for younger groups, especially when there are a number of newer members, and the frequency of rule violations and social inappropriateness or disruptiveness becomes too frequent relative to the capacity of the therapists and other group members to prompt and correct. The best method for using LEGO® Points in the long run is to have them awarded to group members by their peers. This can be prompted by the therapists, but the actual handing over of the points should be left to a peer:

> Dr. Dan: "Jason, did you notice Emily helping Bill so nicely with his project?"
>
> Jason: "Yeah, Dr. Dan, she's a good Helper."
>
> Dr. Dan: "Do you think she deserves a LEGO Point for that?"
>
> Jason: "Yeah, I'd give her two!"
>
> Dr. Dan: "Oh, I think one would be enough, and tell her what it's for."

Over time, the most powerful and consistent reward for collecting a number of LEGO Points for helping out and being a good group member was simply group recognition (social praise, positive peer attention). We also found that it was very effective to allow a group member with the most number of LEGO Points one week to be the *de facto* leader for the group the next week. This was very motivating, since the group member who was most helpful would get to pick the project and be in charge of the activity the next week. Of course, in order to be sure that one group member did not wind up in charge every week, the group leader was exempted from LEGO Points during their reign, but they could certainly assign LEGO Points to others who they found to be helpful and collaborative.

Use of Time-Out

In rare circumstances, a participant may either refuse to comply with a rule, or may persist with being inappropriate or interfering with the group process. Often these situations occur at the beginning or towards the end of the session—during transitions—or following a peer conflict situation. As much as possible, all rule violations and disruptions should be addressed by having peers intervene, and encourage appropriate alternatives, including corrective helpful actions, which could then be recognized with LEGO® Points. Usually just reminding others of the rules is enough. If the behavior does persist, the leader should ask the group members, or a specific group member (usually an experienced group member), how we should address the situation. Only after receiving consensus from other group members should the leader indicate the need for a time-out, often when a child is simply over-stimulated or overly frustrated, and is physically worked up, thereby allowing them time to calm down again.

Time-out consists of being asked to stop their current activity, leave all LEGO pieces, and sit in a remote part of the LEGO room. There is no LEGO nearby, and the group members are not to interact with a participant in time-out, for about five minutes or so. Then, when the participant appears calm and/or eager to rejoin the group, the other participants are asked to discuss the situation with the participant in time-out. Usually, a senior group member will simply ask the participant if he or she understands why they are in time-out, and what they will do differently in similar circumstances in the future. Other group members learn this process by watching senior group members, and may be asked to do the same as they gain more experience in groups.

Often it is a good idea to offer a participant the opportunity to engage in an "act of redemption," in order to compensate the group, and re-establish themselves in good standing with their peers. This can be initiated by a senior group member, or by a participant who may have been offended or inconvenienced by the disruptive member. This should not involve simply saying sorry, but should be some meaningfully helpful gesture or action, such as helping another participant rebuild a broken set, giving another participant a LEGO® Point for being tolerant and forgiving, or allowing another participant to take an expanded role in an ongoing project.

The "Rules of Cool"

Unlike the proscriptive "LEGO Club" Rules, the "Rules of Cool" are implicit, prescriptive rules which are not overtly written or otherwise indicated. These implicit rules are actually defined by the group members as part of an ongoing discussion that takes part during sessions informally. The topic is introduced to members in situations in which members may be inadvertently violating social norms, without necessarily violating one of the "LEGO Club" Rules. Positive, helpful acts exhibited by group members should be noted and pointed out by the therapists or instructors, or have other participants point them out: "Hey, Matt, thanks for sharing with Nick. That was cool. Wasn't that cool, guys?" Encourage other participants to notice and comment on others' actions, especially when they impact on the group activity and communication process: "John, David seems to be talking to the wall. He might be saying something important, but I can't tell. Can you find out what he's talking about? Get him to look at you." Or a conversation might go like this:

Peter: "Arthur, you got your hair cut. I like it."

Arthur: "Yeah? I don't care. I hate it."

Peter: "That wasn't cool. I was trying to give you a compliment."

Arthur: "I still don't care."

Dr. Dan: "Mike, did you hear Arthur? He doesn't care that Peter gave him a compliment about his haircut."

Mike: "Yeah. Arthur's not very cool. He needs to work harder. He'll never have friends."

Dr. Dan: "Peter, did you hear that? Tell him, tell Arthur what Mike said."

Arthur: "I heard him. So what?"

Peter: "Mike said you're not cool, and you'll never have friends."

Arthur: "He said I had to work harder."

Dr. Dan: "Ok, Peter, what does Arthur have to work harder at?"

Peter: "He has to work harder to make friends, by not saying un-cool stuff."

Arthur: "Alright, alright, leave me alone. I just don't like my haircut. I hate getting my hair cut."

Mike: "Yeah, me too. That sucks"

Peter: "Me, three. Ha ha."

The "LEGO® Club" Level System

Similar to many aspects of the LEGO approach, the Level system evolved over time, and was utilized as a strategy to support social development based on direct clinical evidence. The "LEGO® Club" levels are in place to reward children and to motivate children to improve. There are five "LEGO Club" levels, outlined below. Once the skills for a particular level are demonstrated, children are given a "LEGO Club" certificate or diploma, giving the level attained, the date, the location of the "LEGO Club", the therapists, and all participants' names and signatures. These certificates or diplomas are often highly valued, even framed and hung by group members who keep and cherish them for years. Rather than the therapists awarding the certificate, it is the peers in the rest of the group that review whether or not a child's efforts and project meet the specific criteria for a given level. In most groups, however, the therapists need to prompt or remind the group members that a participant has the opportunity to achieve the next level, and that their input is required to help determine if the participant is considered to have qualified for that level. The level requirements are often reviewed (although many group members commit them to memory quickly).

In general, there is a clear and persistent interest by group members in attaining higher levels within the system, and this often leads to improved motivation, task persistence, and willingness to undertake difficult tasks. Some dissension is allowed during the level assignment process—either from the group members or the therapists—but if the arguments against awarding a level are purely *ad hominem*, or the result of some dispute or competitiveness, the therapist can either veto or unilaterally resolve a dispute on the group's behalf. With fairly objective criteria, however, and some coaching from the staff, disagreements about diploma levels are rarely contested. The awarding of a level, especially one of the higher levels, is often a time of celebration for the group and for the parents as well, and often there is a little more "free time" at the end of the session so that the members can enjoy the shared moment of achievement.

1. LEGO® Helper

Participants are considered to be at the Helper level when they first join a group. At this level, they are encouraged to "help out" the group activities by pre-sorting pieces when set-building (e.g. all the gray pieces together), sorting freestyle pieces, checking sets for integrity against directions when completed, ordering, and cleaning the LEGO room. This level serves different functions for children, depending on their skills: for children who are not yet proficient at set-building, or do not have the ability to sustain attention on a task long enough, this allows for participation, and provides the context for peer approval and appreciation of input; for children with higher skills, these activities motivate them to demonstrate their proficiency at higher-level skills in order to move up, including gaining peer approval and building peer alliances.

2. LEGO Builder

Once a LEGO Helper has demonstrated that they can independently construct LEGO sets of a moderate size (100 pieces and above), and can competently fill each of the key roles in the set-building process—Builder, Parts Supplier, and Engineer—in a group set-building activity, the group members will be asked if the participant warrants graduating up to LEGO Builder status. If the group agrees, the participant is then awarded a Builder diploma, which is printed and then signed by the therapist(s) and all other group members.

3. LEGO® Creator

The challenge for a LEGO Builder who wants to move up to being a LEGO Creator is to design, find the parts for, and then construct a freestyle creation. This has to be an original idea, with a certain degree of complexity and gestalt integrity that makes it appealing to the other members. The creation has to clearly be what the Builder had in mind, and have a recognizable form, with some structural integrity and with clear evidence that some thought went into the design. The other group members again make a group decision regarding the creation, and if they are agreed, the participant is given a second diploma.

4. LEGO Master

The challenge at this level is to lead a group project. The participant must have either initiated the group's acquisition of a larger LEGO set (over 300 pieces) for which they then coordinate the construction, or presented to the group a desirable group freestyle project (e.g. build a complex building, a small town, an airport, or a zoo, or construct a series of creations such as a set of vehicles, robots, or other craft). The important point here is that the group members are assigned tasks and roles by the leader, and he effectively directs the project, enlisting support and input from other members, resulting in a project that all group members are agreed was challenging and worthwhile, and was competently led by the Creator/Engineer.

5. *LEGO Genius*

This level was actually created to appease a few LEGO Masters who requested a new challenge against which to pitch their LEGO leadership skills. The criteria for achievement at this level include writing a movie script or story which they present to the group (they can choose a reader for this). The script must be critiqued by other members and edited as necessary. The final script is then analyzed in terms of how the project can be translated into a LEGO® stop-motion animated short film. This is a new development in "LEGO Club" and the details of LEGO stop-action film-making are beyond the scope of this manual, but may be covered in more detail later. The LEGO Master must lead the group in the project, including assigning building tasks for the set and characters, assigning action, voice, and sound-effects roles, controlling or assigning control of the camera and computer (a digital video camera and laptop with editing software are used), and then directing the film itself. The project can take numerous sessions to complete, and requires considerable leadership skill in order to get all members to sustain focus on the task for the required length of time. The resulting animated short film is then edited by the producing member, and is shown to the group, and other groups, and the group members and participants discuss whether the work qualifies as worthy of the LEGO Genius diploma.

LEGO Genius diplomas have also been awarded for very elaborate and involved freestyle creations which display considerable organizational as well as construction and engineering skill, and leadership. For example, one group member designed, and with group support, built a large football stadium, and collected hundreds of mini-figs to be in the stands. He included a bandstand and he created mini-fig replicas of his favorite rock band to play a concert in the stadium. Another participant designed a working elevator which traveled up inside a replica of the Eiffel Tower, and he included smaller buildings and roads, vehicles, and mini-figs throughout, in the cafés and strolling along the sidewalks of Paris.

7

Setting Up Your Own LEGO®-Based Therapy Groups

There are three ways to set up and implement LEGO-Based Therapy:

- *Permanent LEGO Room.* This requires setting up a designated LEGO-Based Therapy room where all the materials are to be kept and where all therapy sessions take place.

- *Temporary Set-Up.* This approach utilizes a specific site, but the materials are not permanently installed or displayed, so that they can be moved or stored separately.

- *Portable Materials.* This involves using a portable set of materials that are transported to different sites (e.g. schools, community settings, libraries).

Note that these different approaches are not mutually exclusive, and we have used all three depending on the circumstances. There are advantages and disadvantages to each approach, and the decision regarding which would be most appropriate depends on a number of factors that are discussed in Table 7.1.

Permanent LEGO® Room

The first site-specific and permanent LEGO room was not so much a result of planning, as of natural evolution. Initially, LEGO materials were available in a play therapy room which also included a range of other materials. Over time, however, the participants themselves chose to focus on LEGO-Based activities, and the other materials were either co-opted into use with LEGO (e.g. using painting materials to create backdrops for LEGO scenes; using the sand-tray and water-table to create specialized settings for LEGO creations) or simply pushed out of the way. Once the term "LEGO Club" was applied to the room, there was no going back.

An exclusive, dedicated LEGO space gives the participants a strong sense of group identification, and a more immediate response to the possibility of becoming a "member" of the "LEGO Club." Motivation to participate in group activities, and to follow behavioral and social rules, are important factors in effective social skills interventions. Most of the children who have participated in "LEGO Clubs" appear to be relieved that the group activities are so clearly prescribed, as well as excited ("All we do is build LEGO? I can do that!").

Physical Layout

A key aspect of creating a successful LEGO room is the physical layout. The LEGO room should be visually stimulating and inviting, without being overwhelming. In order to achieve this, it is important to provide a balance of complexity with visual order (a characteristic of LEGO materials themselves). The LEGO room must be set up in such a way so that the materials are evident and accessible, without being overwhelming. Use of display shelves and tables, with orderly displays of both freestyle creations and

LEGO® sets (arranged by theme, preferably), is encouraged. These should not be overly cluttered, and must be well-secured (we had one incident involving a large, unsecured shelving unit loaded with LEGO and a visiting two-year-old, which kept the group busy sorting and rebuilding sets for weeks). Freestyle display areas should be physically separate from set displays. The display areas should be around the outside of the room, with the center of the LEGO room reserved for the LEGO building surfaces and materials. As much as possible, keep the structure and design of the LEGO room consistent and predictable, but with enough spare surface or display area for growth and new projects.

Very complex display sets should be stored out of reach of younger participants. This inevitably results in attempts to climb shelves, and this tendency should be addressed proactively (see "'LEGO® Club' Rules" in Chapter 6). Simpler, "hands-on" sets can be displayed on lower shelves. It is acceptable, and expected, that these sets will be manipulated, and dismantled frequently. The shelves should be sturdy enough to withstand frequent contact, and be free from dangerous edges and materials: wood or plastic shelves tend to work best. Keep in mind that the shelves will need to be deep enough to accommodate larger sets.

The use of a limited number of primary colors in both wall colors and furniture tends to emphasize the LEGO-specific quality of the space, and decreases over-stimulation. Our current LEGO room is painted in large blocks of LEGO colors—the colors of LEGO bricks were easily duplicated at the hardware store. The lighting needs to be adequate for careful examination of the materials and directions, but also soft enough to reduce glare (typically, fluorescent lighting with frosted diffusion panels).

There should be two visibly separate centers in the LEGO room: one for set-building and one for freestyle creating. The set-building area should have only those materials related to ongoing set projects. Overlapping freestyle and set-building tends to lead to degradation of the sets, that is, unauthorized borrowing (see "'LEGO® Club' Rules" in Chapter 6). The set-building area should be large enough to accommodate the full group, with close arrangement of seating. The best set-up for this we've found is the standard teacher's jelly-bean-shaped instruction table. During set-building, it is best to try to keep the participants seated, and not on top of each other, as this tends to decrease compliance with tasks and increases conflicts.

The freestyle building area should be the most accessible in the LEGO room, and there should be easily accessible bins of materials. The projects tend to be more collaborative, with less order, and remaining seated is not always necessary or appropriate. Participants tend to roam around the project to get access to materials, and the leader will be challenged by the many opportunities for corrective feedback regarding nonverbal communication. The freestyle display area should also be elevated, with a lower shelf for younger-member creations, and a higher shelf for more ambitious projects. Never underestimate the importance of a personal creation, nor the memory span of its creator.

In one corner of the LEGO room, place a large armchair. This chair is often used by adults when they visit the LEGO room, but is designated within group sessions as "The time-out chair." This chair is used only in unusual circumstances, such as persistent or flagrant rule violation, interpersonal aggression, tantrums, or for persistent over-arousal ("the sillies"). Use of time-out is discussed in Chapter 6.

Establishing the Structure

The LEGO® room should always be in good order and with evident attention to detail. The impact of a visually disorganized room is immediately apparent in the behavior of the participants. In a well-organized room, the participants are likely to be more inhibited in their initial approach, but they are also more likely to take the responsibility of maintaining the LEGO room more seriously. Before a new member or visitor is allowed to work with or examine the materials, they should be given an orientation to the LEGO room, and the rules.

Emphasize the group cohesiveness and identity by restricting access to non-members, such as siblings and parents. In some instances, siblings are included as members, but generally they are allowed into the LEGO room briefly only when invited by participants. Although this can create sibling conflicts, the harm is usually outweighed by the benefits of peer-group identification.

The rules for the group should be prominently displayed. There should be at least one large and accessible cork or other display board. This should contain the rules, as well as photos, drawings, and so on which group members use to display. It is also used for rehearsing group members' names, and for visual cueing regarding social rehearsal during individual therapy sessions.

Keep to the schedule of the group carefully. Do not allow participants into the LEGO room before the group time, and have the group members leave on time. Both of these require considerable attention and planning as there tends to be a strong pressure to enter and stay in the LEGO room—this is less of a problem with temporary or portable materials. Beginning and ending the group on time helps with implementing social rules (greetings and salutations, learning names, etc.), as well as allaying anxieties. Inevitably, participants arrive early or late. Both situations can be opportunities for peer-mediated coping, and some coaching of parents about waiting-room behavior can help considerably. For those who have a lot of LEGO® at home, it is good to have them bring in photographs of their favorite creations, and share them with the group. This might also create opportunities for off-shoot activities, such as sleep-overs and LEGO birthday parties. If a participant has a better LEGO room at home, he will opt out of the social learning so it may be necessary to entice him with the most exciting collection he has ever seen.

Temporary Set-Up

The multipurpose site tends not to be as effective in creating a motivation to participate, or in encouraging group identity and cohesion, but it can be an effective alternative to a permanent site. The emphasis on structure and routine is even more important, as well as the use of support materials, such as photographs, LEGO literature, and display boards. As much as possible, set up the room using the guidelines above, and try to keep the same furniture arrangement from session to session. Close arrangement of seating is necessary to encourage close interaction during set-building, while more open arrangements or standing up around a table can be useful during freestyle building and creative play. Emphasize the social unit by noticing when members are absent, and the importance of roles within the group. The following specific recommendations may be helpful:

- Use portable or temporary support materials (poster boards with photographs of members and favorite projects).

- Ensure the presence of LEGO® publications, posters, etc.

- Emphasize consistent attendance, and routine within the sessions.

- Create group structure and social roles (e.g. election of "LEGO Club" officers; hierarchy of LEGO Helpers, Builders, Creators, etc.).

- Use the same location, even if it is a multipurpose site.

- When possible, use multi-session projects (i.e. large sets or other projects requiring multiple sessions for completion).

Portable Materials

Although it might seem that creating a structure and group cohesion would be especially difficult when visiting a site with portable materials, this is not always the case. Part of the benefit of going to a school or other site is that it emphasizes the uniqueness of the group and its members relative to the rest of the population. This can sometimes create problems of its own, as non-members or parents at the site may request participation. This problem has been resolved at times by having others participate as Helpers (reverse inclusion), but there may be difficulties arising from, for example, confidentiality and consent, especially in mental health settings.

One of the drawbacks of portable "LEGO® Clubs" is often inadequate or inappropriate space allocation (we've conducted "LEGO Clubs" in storage rooms many times), or lack of an enclosed space altogether (e.g. middle of a library). Working with school or other facility administrators in advance to find or set up an appropriate space is well worth the time and effort. This should include a discussion of possible storage space, and use of selected school materials (e.g. display boards, tables and chairs, shelving). Schools and other facilities often have assigned rooms for speech-language or occupational therapy, and these are excellent possible sites, when available.

The other potential stumbling block in this situation is uninformed site staff. The intrusion of other staff into the group can be disruptive both to the ongoing process as well as to the less obvious group identification issues. Preparing site staff with a quick briefing and establishing procedures with them prior to starting group or individual sessions is important. Although most school or facility staff recognize the confidential, nature of individual therapy, they may not see this in the context of a "play group." When considering which set-up system to follow, it might be helpful to consider the factors outlined in Table 7.1.

Table 7.1 Factors in choosing the LEGO®-Based Therapy group set-up

1. Who the group is for	In some instances, the group participants may not have the option of traveling to a designated site, as in hospitalized children or otherwise non-ambulatory children. There may also be a mix of participants for whom the materials would need to be changed or moved. For example, an assigned space may be shared between participants across a wide age range. Consequently, some LEGO materials would present a risk for younger children (as well as a risk to the materials), while older participants may not identify with and appreciate the presence of early childhood materials.
2. How many people and how many groups	As the number of participants increases, there is a greater demand for physical structure in the set-up of the therapy space, and that limits the feasibility of portable interventions. Also, with higher numbers of groups, the requirement for more varied LEGO materials, and support materials (shelves, storage containers, table-top space), usually requires a designated room.
3. Geographical location	When the group participants are close to each other but far from the leader, it is often easier to have the therapist bring materials to the group setting. This is often the case when group members are all students at one school or residents in a program, which may be some distance from the leader's home-base.
4. Availability of space	In many instances, the leader may not have access to an appropriate space which can be set up as a permanent LEGO room. In this case, although a single room might be used on a regular basis for therapy sessions, the materials may need to be stored or removed from the space. This is usually the situation in public school settings.

cont.

Table 7.1 Factors in choosing the LEGO®-Based Therapy group set-up *continued*

5. The time–space continuum	One of the chronic difficulties involved in using the LEGO room approach is room availability. This is especially critical when the site is in a clinic or office where children are typically coming on an out-patient basis and are not available during normal business hours because of school. There are a limited number of hours in the day during which children can feasibly be seen after school. Both for the sake of efficacy and the mental health of the leader, running groups later in the evening is not recommended. Running simultaneous groups can maximize resources, although this usually requires that at least one of the groups be a temporary one. See Sharing, below.
6. Sharing	For schools, clinics and other institutions, it is cost-effective to have multiple leaders share a set of LEGO materials. This can be achieved with any of the set-up options, and different set-ups can be combined; for example, a sub-set of materials can be removed from a permanent room for use in another site. This allows for simultaneous groups, which we have previously done, with good results, especially in terms of resource allocation. Portable set-ups are easily shared, but are not effective for simultaneous use. Having a central storage area which can be accessed by multiple leaders is a good option, although with this approach the integrity of the materials tends to decline due to "diffusion of responsibility" effects.
7. Scheduling	Finding a meeting time which accommodates the schedules of parents, participants, and siblings, including travel to and from the group or individual sessions, has been a significant problem. A number of "LEGO Clubs" have stopped meeting entirely as a result of inconsistent attendance due primarily to scheduling conflicts. This seems especially to be a factor for older participants who are more likely to have additional after-school activities and commitments. This headache is obviated by having groups on-site at a school or hospital, and parents especially are often very appreciative of this option.

8. Choice and flexibility	The permanent LEGO room has the advantage of having more materials and a broader range of activities than can be accommodated in a temporary or portable set-up. This allows for important group decision-making opportunities, and gives more of a sense of ownership and self-direction to the group members. Although more than one activity can be accommodated by either temporary or portable materials, this is much more limited.
9. Group identity and cohesion	Part of the effectiveness of this approach is based on creating a sense of group cohesion and identity. For many participants, the "LEGO Club" is the first social activity with which they actively identify, and in which they enthusiastically participate. Most of the children who benefit from this therapy do not easily identify with others, and have deficits in empathy. Consequently, creating a physical setting which supports and facilitates group cohesion and social belonging can be a necessary component. The absence of group identification in some children was highlighted by one of my participants who never responded to general instructions given to the group, for example "Okay, everybody, it's time to clean up." When asked why he was not helping to clean up, he responded, "You said everybody, not me!" In this regard, the permanent LEGO room has distinct advantages, and temporary or portable approaches need to compensate for this shortcoming in other ways.
10. Third-party payer issues	Although the costs of participation in this form of intervention are often covered by school districts, either directly or through contracted services, many of the participants in the US have utilized private health insurance to cover individual and group therapy sessions. Due to the nature of third-party payer contracts, services are required to be provided at a designated site. Although this does not preclude one from having a temporary use of space, it does preclude travel to another site, unless, in some instances, the site is a hospital or residential mental health clinic.

cont.

Table 7.1 Factors in choosing the LEGO®-Based Therapy group set-up *continued*

11. Integrity of materials	Anyone who has ever attempted to transport a LEGO creation in a moving vehicle will agree that portability has its limitations. This becomes a factor especially with larger, more complex projects which require multiple sessions to complete. Nothing is more disappointing to a group of participants than a set-back resulting from travel damage. If at all possible, the materials should be safely stored on-site. The LEGO pieces themselves are very resilient for the most part (there are a few minor exceptions), but the support materials (magazines and catalogues, display materials, etc.) are not. Again, on-site storage is a good option.
12. Graft	Although it has always been a pleasant surprise to us that there is usually very little in the way of informal "borrowing," there are some factors that seem to increase the risk of this. First, newcomers or visitors to the room or site seem to be much more tempted than regular group members. Second, the degree of visible organization and structure of the room helps, likely because the missing elements would be immediately apparent (at least to those familiar with the room or set-up)—portable or temporary materials are at a much higher risk than those in a fixed setting. Third, group size and adult-to-participant ratio is a factor. With a ratio of less than 1:3 or 1:4, the graft risk increases significantly. With 1:5 or more, somewhat depending on participant characteristics, the leader will likely need to institute graft-reduction technique.
13. Displays	One of the more important features of the "LEGO Club" experience is the pride in creativity and skill inherent in displaying sets and creations. This seems to be universal, regardless of the level of skill or complexity involved. The sharing of creations with parents and siblings, as well as the more individualistic self-efficacy, are both enhanced by having more or less permanent reminders. Both parents and participants have expressed considerable benefit from the mutual activity of showing and being shown the LEGO projects. Although the display component can be accommodated to some degree in temporary set-ups using photographs (preferably digital, so that the images can be displayed immediately), there is a loss of immediacy and the degree of excitement involved in "Look what I just made!" There is also a lingering pride associated with "Yeah, I remember making that." Perhaps most importantly, the admiration of one's peers seems to be especially valuable in building self-confidence and self-efficacy. "Did you make that? Wow!"

8

Specific Materials and Arrangements

Choosing Materials: Sets with Instructions

The choice of materials is a key issue in implementing LEGO®-Based interventions, for obvious reasons. Unlike many other approaches, however, the process of choosing the materials is an integral part of the therapy itself. Participant selection of LEGO materials can be a part of both individual and group therapy sessions, and should be both structured and facilitated by the therapist.

When you are starting off, it is useful to have some LEGO sets already, and some ideas of LEGO sets that have been popular are listed in Table 8.1. Bear in mind that a part of LEGO-Based Therapy is that, wherever possible, the children choose models themselves and discuss as a group which models to get. You should talk to children individually to find out what sort of LEGO they enjoy and find motivating. You can do this by showing children LEGO magazines or LEGO catalogues, or by looking at the LEGO website (www.lego.com). All LEGO models have an age range and the number of pieces specified. In general, the fewer the pieces, the cheaper the model and the faster they are to build.

Table 8.1 Popular LEGO® sets

LEGO Model	Age range	Number of pieces
Mini astro-fighter	6–12	57
Police car 7236	5+	59
Mini construction 4915	6–12	68
Fire helicopter 7238	5+	75
Ambulance 7890	5–12	118
Digger 7248	5+	127
Fireboat 7906	5–12	187
Cool cars 7245	6–12	206
Passenger plane 7893	5–12	401
Mobile crane 7249	6+	524
Police station 7237	5+	597
Ferrari 8145	10–16	1327

When children are choosing LEGO models, bear in mind that LEGO comes in several different themes that might be popular with children. Table 8.2 shows a list of the themes available at the time of writing this manual. In addition, for older, more experienced Builders, there is LEGO Technic® and LEGO Mindstorms®. There is also a LEGO factory online that is free to use, where you can custom-design your own model and get the bricks to build it.

Table 8.2 Popular LEGO themes

Bionicle®	City®	Harry Potter®	Belville (girls)®	Exoforce®	Sports®
Castle®	Aqua Raiders®	Batman®	Racers®	Trains®	Lego Trains®
Mars Mission®	Star Wars®	Sponge Bob®	Vikings®	Ferrari®	Bob-the-Builder®

In individual therapy, access to specific new LEGO® sets or building materials can be made contingent on targeted behavioral goals. The goals can be agreed upon and monitored by the participants themselves, or by report from either parents or teachers. Integration of individual and group sessions is also often achieved by having participants practice a persuasive argument with the therapist, and then introduce this proposal to the group for consideration. Social communication can be coached and prompted in both individual and group therapy. The success of this technique often rests on the level of motivation for acquisition of the new set. There is little risk that the participant will neglect to initiate communication if it is clear that his initiating group discussion and consensus is a prerequisite for getting the coveted new LEGO.

It is best to establish a specific budget with both individuals and groups. This often creates a press among members to have more of the Club funds utilized for their particular interest, and the resulting conflict can be very fruitful for coaching social problem-solving, sharing, turn-taking, and reciprocity. Effective social communication can be enhanced by individual coaching, as well as by prompting during group sessions. Encourage group members to express reluctance or lack of interest for another's ideas openly, and assertively, but appropriately. Although the process can be frustrating for those with communication deficits, their motivation will be high. Turn-taking in presenting conflicting points of view, with rebuttals and counter-arguments, can significantly improve social communication, and this tends to be generalized. Language functioning has been shown to account for some of the variance in overall treatment outcome, however, and concomitant speech-language therapy is important.

Choosing Materials: Freestyle LEGO®

Freestyle LEGO materials can be acquired either directly from LEGO or acquired informally as the remnants of defunct sets, donated shoeboxes full of abandoned bits, or in large bins or sets which have multiple possible uses. As much as possible, the freestyle materials should be kept organized in plastic, see-through bins. A large supply of freestyle materials is needed in order to facilitate the wide range of interests, and the tendency for group members to reify freestyle creations. Although members can be encouraged to "recycle" freestyle pieces, certain ground-breaking masterpieces tend to take on particular importance for all concerned. A large supply of freestyle materials can be acquired by donations, although these often require extensive sorting and cleaning, which is time-consuming. LEGO Educational Division also offers a large range at reduced cost to educational and non-profit organizations.

Maintaining Materials

In order to get a group started, the leader will need to have a core set of materials that will facilitate both set-building and freestyle activities. Sets are readily available at retail outlets or through online sources (http://shop.lego.com), and the best information regarding available products is on the LEGO website and in catalogues. Display sets are often useful in getting group members interested in participating. A critical factor in the long-range success of a "LEGO Club" is retaining set directions. Keep these in a safe, separate location that can be accessed but not easily trampled or rummaged. A large drawer, or box placed on a shelf, will do.

LEGO sets on display rarely survive more than a few days without significant alteration, if not complete disassembly.

The consistent application of Rule #1—"If you break it, you have to fix it"—is a necessary though not sufficient rule for sustaining an orderly and effective set of materials. In addition to resorting to Rule #2—"If you can't fix it, ask for help"—there may also be some special clean-up sessions, and restoration projects. When a set is restored, it is often necessary to disassemble it completely first in order to follow the direction sequence. This is a good opportunity to replace or repair parts, and to clean the parts. LEGO® pieces tend to collect dust (in part because of all the handling), and this can make the sets look old and neglected before their time (we have some LEGO sets that are 15 years old or older, and still look like new, and are treated by the participants as new, because the plastic is bright, and not dusty). Dusting is best done with a clean toothbrush, or similar non-abrasive plastic brush.

Another key factor in maintaining LEGO in good condition is the strict adherence to the "No teeth" rule. Never let members attempt to separate parts with their teeth. Aside from the obvious hygiene issue and risk of damaged teeth (especially among six- and seven-year-olds), it permanently damages the material, as few other things will. Some older white LEGO pieces will yellow with age, but most colored bricks retain their new look for decades.

Whenever a set structure is damaged or temporarily modified, all the set pieces should be collected and placed in a tray (we use colorful cafeteria trays as well as plastic see-through tubs). We also use trays during initial set construction. This facilitates searching for parts, while reducing (not eliminating) the number of pieces on the floor. During clean-up at the end of each session, be sure to do a thorough floor search (many small LEGO pieces have been saved from the vacuum cleaner this way).

The maintenance of the materials in presentable order often falls on the older participants, as the younger ones tend to have less focus and skill, as well as poorer impulse control. Although this often results in the older members creating a mock fuss about having to fix disassembled sets, there is also a tendency for group members to bond with each other over this issue, and to create a heightened sense of group cohesion.

9

Assessment Procedures

A key component of any intervention is thorough assessment. The assessment process allows the leader to determine areas of need and strength, and to establish objective baseline data for assessing progress in future. The assessment process has two elements: the initial assessment; and progress assessment. Although there will be considerable variability across leaders and individual participants, the following general guidelines have been established as core features of LEGO®-Based Therapies through both clinical experience and research.

Initial Assessment

Initial Interview

The assessment process should begin with an introductory interview of the participant and family, typically one hour. This interview is designed both to provide information regarding the methodology and procedures to participants and parents, and to collect information about the participant that will help with further assessment and treatment planning. If the leader will be using a permanent LEGO room site, then the interview should be conducted in that room and the interview will begin with an orientation to the room. If the site is a temporary one (multipurpose room), then the LEGO materials should be present. Otherwise, if the participant will be attending a portable site, the interview can be conducted at the site, or at the leader's clinic or office.

In any case, it is helpful for information-sharing, as well as for establishing rapport, to have LEGO® materials available at the initial interview.

The interview should be conducted in a relatively informal and unstructured manner. References to the mental health aspects of LEGO intervention should be minimized (e.g. therapy, interventions, diagnoses, social skills), with an emphasis on the activities, requirements for participation, and the social nature of the group.

Important information to be shared with participants and parents at the initial interview, which is typically one hour, includes the following:

- consent/assent procedures and confidentiality issues

- audiovisual recording, and consent procedures, if any

- frequency, duration, and location of group and individual therapy sessions

- opportunities for family involvement

- group and individual therapy modalities

- costs or third-party payer arrangements

- attendance expectations and cancellation procedures

- "LEGO Club" Rules

- LEGO-Based Therapy methodology

- brief review of outcome studies and efficacy of methodology

- expected benefits and methods for assessing outcome

- "LEGO Club" level system (i.e. Helper, Builder, Creator, Master, and Genius)

- termination planning, that is, "Graduation"

- alternative and/or additional interventions that may be beneficial.

Most of this information is conveyed directly to parents during the interview. It is also helpful to have written information, in the form of a brochure or single-page description, which may be shared with parents and educators either at the initial interview or beforehand. Many parents find this helpful as there is often too much information to absorb in one interview. The participant should be directly involved in the discussion of the "LEGO® Club" Rules, and asked if they understand and can comply with the rules as a condition of participation.

During the interview, usually while parents are providing information based on the Intake Assessment semi-structured interview (see Appendix A), the participant is offered two LEGO activities which will provide direct information regarding the participant's skills and behaviors. The interviewer will be required to do both the interview and informal observation simultaneously, unless there are two individuals conducting the interview. Interviewers are encouraged to utilize the structured observation form, provided in Appendix B.

Building a Small Set

In a LEGO Room setting, it may be difficult to get the participant to focus on building as they are often distracted by exploring the displayed sets and creations. Allow them to explore for a few minutes, and then say, "I need your help. Do you think you can put this together for me?" The interviewer should provide a small set, ranging from 20–30 pieces to up to roughly 100 pieces, depending on the age and developmental level of the child. For most participants, a small to medium-sized vehicle with a wind-up motor, or a small airplane, are good choices as they are highly motivating, and there are many small and large versions of these available. The set should be completely disassembled, presented on a holding tray, with the instructions. The interviewer should continue the interview with the parent, and unobtrusively observe the following:

- Does the child comply with the request appropriately and independently?

- Does the child request help in completing the set or do so independently?

- Does the child make eye contact and engage in other appropriate social communication in response to the interviewer?

- Is the child able to complete the task easily, or with difficulty?

- Is the set completed correctly?

- Does the child follow the directions in a step-wise fashion, or do they jump ahead, or complete the set without following the directions?

- Does the child modify the set or make something completely novel?

- Does the child show the end results to the interviewer or parent(s) when done, or do they simply leave the set aside and move on?

- Does the child maintain contact by verbal or nonverbal communication while building?

Freestyle Building

After presenting the participant with the small set, the interviewer should invite them to utilize freestyle materials to build their own creation. Freestyle materials should include both large and small building pieces, architectural as well as vehicle components, human figures, and aircraft or spacecraft elements. The following should be noted by informal observation:

- What is the extent and duration of preparation—that is, evidence of planning versus impulsivity?

- What is the organization and structure of the results: again, is there evidence of form and planning, or is it poorly constructed and chaotic?

- Is there evidence of a theme or predominant obsessive interest?

- Does the child request help with either ideas or construction?

- Does the child decide on a design, or do they change frequently, or change how they label or describe the creation frequently?

- How long does the child sustain focus independently on this task?

- Does the child show pride and request social approval following the task?

- Are they able to stop when requested or do they insist on continuing to build at the end of the interview?

- Do they exhibit any inappropriate behaviors related to frustration during building or in transitioning from the task?

Initial Observation in a Natural Setting

In addition to the initial interview and structured observations, the initial assessment process should include direct observation of the participant in a typical social setting. This has typically been done on the playground or in a group social setting at school, during recess or lunch break. The observation can be done by the leader or by a teacher or other adult capable of doing structured observation.

There are three targeted areas for observation, two of which are uniform across participants, and one which requires some individualized definition of the problem (operationalization), which is based on the initial interview and observations. The first target is frequency of self-initiated social contact. This is defined as follows: "Number of times per 15-minute whole interval in which the child spontaneously approaches a peer, and initiates interaction, either by verbal or nonverbal communication, offering to share something, initiating joint attention, or by physical contact." The contact is not counted if it is prompted by an adult, based on a prior contingency arrangement, or if the child is approached by a peer. It is counted if the peer approaches the participant after the participant gestures or otherwise communicates with them, but then the peer delays response. If an interaction is interrupted or stops and the participant re-contacts the same peer, this is also counted.

The second target for observation is duration of social interaction. This is defined as follows: "Total amount of time during which the child is engaged in social interaction with peers without adult direction or supervision, during a 15-minute whole interval." The interaction can include parallel play, but must be within close proximity (i.e. less than two feet), and include some clear signs of joint attention or nonverbal communication. The interaction can be prompted or initiated by either an adult or a peer, but the recording of duration should include only non-supervised interaction. The total duration of interaction is divided by the number of interactions, giving the average length of social interaction.

The third target area is the frequency of stereotyped movements and potentially stigmatizing mannerisms, gestures, or habits. Since this varies considerably across individuals, and there is usually more than one per participant, the definition of these features is left up to the leader, family, and educators. Typical examples include: engaging in stereotyped movements gestures, such as hand-flapping or repeatedly touching a body part (ears, eyes, nose, hair, etc.); pacing; odd body postures; inappropriate touching or inappropriate intrusion into personal space; preoccupation with certain features of the LEGO room (doors, locks, light switches), or preoccupation with other objects, either their own or those belonging to the "LEGO® Club" (e.g. string, chain, wire, flat shiny surfaces, writing instruments, small vehicles, wheels, fans, drawers); mouthing objects; hiding or hoarding objects. In this category, the total number of occurrences of the identified gesture or habit is recorded during the whole interval of a 15-minute play period.

For older participants who do not have recess, these observations may need to be made during another unstructured activity at school (lunch, library, PE), during after-school activities (study hall), or, failing other options, during a "LEGO Club."

Follow-up Assessments

For purposes of progress tracking and treatment planning, it is essential to have at least annual re-assessments, including interviews of parents, feedback from teachers, and repeated observations in natural settings. The use of standardized assessment instruments, such as the Wechsler intelligence tests, neuropsychological batteries, and adaptive rating scales (e.g. Vineland-II; Sparrow, Cicchetti, and Balla 2005), are recommended for objective progress tracking, in addition to use of rating scales such as the Gilliam ASC Rating Scale® (GARS-3; Gilliam 2013) or the Gilliam Asperger Disorder Scale® (GADS; Gilliam 2001). The authors have also used the Vineland Adaptive Behavior Scales, Second Edition (Vineland-II; Sparrow *et al.* 2005) Socialization Domain as a measure of overall social development and adjustment (LeGoff and Sherman 2006). This can be filled out by either parents or teachers by interview. It is relatively brief, has computerized scoring, and has well-developed norms for all age groups, including adults. The best overall indicators of social adjustment and development, however, are the direct observational measures.

In this regard, it is important to keep observations consistent over time (i.e. use of the same raters, and same rating criteria), using the same settings and events. Improvements on one of the observed variables without commensurate gains on the others can indicate problems with generalization of gains, or with the intervention itself. At times, there may be interfering factors, such as persistent and frequent stigmatizing behaviors (e.g. thumb-sucking, scripting) that may require additional, focal intervention.

The research on LEGO® interventions has indicated that increased frequency of self-initiated social contact tends to level off before the other two measures (LeGoff 2004), although all three measures have inherent floor and ceiling effects. There is also a tendency for duration of contact to be inversely proportional to frequency of contact. Once these measures begin to become unreliable or invalid as measures of social competence, other objective measures should be substituted. This is often the case with older participants. In this case, the use of the Vineland Adaptive Behavior Scales (Vineland-II; Sparrow *et al.* 2005) or other ratings of social adaptation may yield more valid results, with fewer ceiling effects.

The candidate can also be observed in the group sessions themselves. Objective measures of the frequency of appropriate social initiations, or any specific areas you want to work on, can be developed in order to assess ongoing progress or lack thereof. It is important to specify exactly what constitutes the target you are measuring so that it can be coded accurately by any trained observer of the groups. It is helpful to videotape children in the situations you want to observe them. This means that you can come up with consensus codes for targeted actions and review sessions at a later time.

Termination/Graduation

The long-term outcome and "graduation" from the "LEGO® Club" is based on indicators of age-appropriate peer relationships. Typically, this takes the form of involvement in after-school social activities with peers, establishment of peer friendships, and loss of focus on the "LEGO Club" as the center of social activity for the participant. Therapists are encouraged to have consistent periodic meetings with families to discuss progress and termination/graduation. Including the participant in these discussions is important, although one must be careful to avoid negative impact of termination effects (i.e. self-sabotaging strategies to avoid graduation). For this reason, participants and families have often been given an "open door" policy post-graduation: the participant is always welcome to return for visits as a "Helper." The number of post-graduation visits is usually very low, and there have not been problems with abuse of this policy to date. The returning former participants are often identified to the current participants as one of the "LEGO® Legends." Graduated members often seem pleased and honored to be identified as a graduate, and now Legend, of the "LEGO Club."

Presenting graduates with a brief ceremony and diploma has become one of the "LEGO Club's" more cherished traditions. Other group members are often strongly motivated to graduate as well, and are keen to achieve higher "LEGO Club" status as they demonstrate improved technical and social competence.

10

Experiences of Running "LEGO® Clubs"

Sixteen Suggestions for Running "LEGO Clubs" Smoothly

(From 16 years of experience running "LEGO Clubs," which were often anything but smooth.)

1. Select candidate members carefully in terms of compatibility of age, developmental level, diagnosis, and so on. Follow the intake procedures in the manual, but also just get to know the candidates a bit, and get a sense of whether they would be a "good fit" with the others.

2. Develop consistent lines of communication with parents and expect to spend time with them before and after groups, but, unfortunately, they should not be included or allowed to observe groups (unless it's unobtrusive, like a one-way mirror or videotaping). Parental presence inhibits the social bonding and the sense of Club-ness.

3. Don't refer to the "LEGO Club" as therapy to the participants, and encourage parents to refrain from calling it therapy or social skills. It's just the "LEGO Club."

4. Be vigilant about making sure everyone is participating in small-group, dyad, or triad activities. Not solo. Many members will try to pass off parallel play as a group activity. It's not. "LEGO® Club" participation requires interdependent, interactive, and communicative engagement with peers.

5. In this regard, make sure the child not participating is doing so because they're just aloof and self-absorbed, not anxious and overwhelmed. If they are really socially anxious, transition them towards working with a supportive, considerate peer by initially having them work with an adult, then an adult and one peer, and then just the peer.

6. Highlight the achievements—take pictures and put them up in the LEGO room or post them on a members-only website (i.e. secure site) or similar. Make sure the pictures are of the group. Build a group identity. Be careful to ensure that all members and parents have consented to this, however, and be aware of all confidentiality issues involved.

7. Make sure your therapists or adult staff don't help too much. This is a common problem. If the kids are doing their thing and all is going well, just sit back, or participate minimally. Facilitate, don't interfere, unless you have to, and don't get caught up in the LEGO-building projects. That's the focus for the participants. The therapists should focus on the communication and interaction.

8. Don't impose artificial social rules, like shaking hands or introducing themselves by name. As indicated above, observation of typical kids of similar ages can be helpful in discerning age, gender, and culturally

specific and current norms. Don't expect social norms to remain constant over multiple generations (look what happened to nod).

9. As age ranges near puberty, try not to mix pre- and post-pubertal kids. They're from different worlds. Enough said.

10. Girls do great in "LEGO® Clubs," but they may need some additional support and encouragement especially if they are the only girl. Let them show their talents, and take some leadership.

11. Don't let one or two kids dominate the group. Address that as soon as it starts to happen by encouraging other kids to take the lead, give ideas, and be in charge of projects.

12. If some participants have limited skills with building, make sure they have Helper tasks (sorting or finding pieces, etc.), and highlight the benefit of these important Helpers.

13. Have the kids come up with their own proscriptive rules ("LEGO Club" Rules) and prescriptive rules (Rules of Cool). Therapy staff should be highlighting the pro-social, helpful actions. Notice and comment on helping, sharing, communication, and so on. If the participants want adult help in social conflicts, or even with the LEGO projects, deflect it back to the group. Have them help each other as much as possible.

14. Ensure that parents and participants are clear about attendance expectations, and have clear rules regarding non-attendance. Make sure parents or the participant informs staff in advance of non-

attendance, if possible, for example during vacations, family trips, changes in schedule.

15. Keep a waiting list of participants for each group who would be appropriate to join an ongoing group once a group member stops attending, either as a drop-out or graduate. Scheduling and attendance is much less of an issue for groups which occur at school during school hours; however, vacations or other absences may also occur, and need to be anticipated.

16. Be careful about hygiene rules, especially during the cold/flu season. Since the group members and staff are all in close proximity, and are handling the same materials for prolonged periods, washing hands before and after sessions, and periodically washing the LEGO® materials themselves, are reasonable precautions, in addition to having hand-sanitizer and tissues available in the LEGO room (especially when someone comes to group sessions with a cold or other symptoms of a potentially infectious virus).

My Experience of Running "LEGO Clubs"
Ruth Howard, Regional Officer, National Autistic Society

What do you wish you had known before starting groups?

Tricky one! I think that I would say to spend a lot of time and consideration on placing/matching the young people into groups. We were always careful to ensure social and communication abilities were around the same level, but it is very important to ensure that the young people "click" with each other initially as this has a significant impact upon the success and achievements.

Do you have any "top tips" for professionals about to set up their own groups?

- Keep in mind that it is not about the LEGO® but social skills and communication development! The LEGO helps young people to be motivated enough to join and enjoy the group, but this is to facilitate the development of skills. It is very easy to lose sight of this when running a group.

- When there is opportunity to help young people to deal with social issues, it is important to help them work out a solution or response themselves. It's all too easy to jump in and offer the solution, but this does not help them to gain the skills for the future and can be disempowering.

- We found it important to ensure that the young people experienced success and completion of a project during each session. We found it can be very easy to underestimate the length of time it can take to complete a small LEGO kit in early sessions when the young people are getting used to each other, and how LEGO groups work. It is better to have a very small project that is completed with time spare to socialise, than to not complete the project as this can lead to frustration and disappointment.

- Be positive! Participating in a "LEGO Club" is very challenging for anyone, but the challenges that young people face lead to great opportunities for learning and development and should not be seen as a disaster!

Qualitative Research Exploring Children's Experience of LEGO®-Based Therapy

Elinor Brett, trainee Educational Psychologist, University of Exeter, UK

Elinor Brett carried out a qualitative study of children's experiences of "LEGO Clubs" run in mainstream primary schools in Cambridge (Brett 2013). She used semi-structured interviews to identify what features of LEGO-Based Therapy were interesting and engaging for children and which elements children found more challenging.

Children found the groups very enjoyable:

> "It just really starts my week off well and makes me really really happy. Yeah, I just wake up and know it's a really nice day and I get to school and "LEGO Club" just makes my day really good."

They found working with others, forming new friendships, and belonging to a team to be motivating:

> "It's not just about me building, it's about everyone building. I like being in a team."

> "...'cos when you're doing it by your own you're quite bored aren't you but when you're together it's quite fun."

> "Well, we got to know more about each other and we got to do stuff together."

Freestyle LEGO® building where children create their own models in small groups or pairs was also really popular:

> "Because you got to build whatever you liked pretty much. We tried to build a city but we only built four things so it was more like a hamlet."

Children were drawn to LEGO and spoke positively and enthusiastically about it, particularly due to its infinite creative opportunities:

> "My favourite thing about LEGO is that there's about a jillion pieces of LEGO in the world. It's like you can build anything you want with it because there's just so much pieces."

Children also felt skilled at LEGO building, which bolstered their self-esteem:

> "Well, I find it quite easy to build very hard stuff. Like I could probably build a chair."

While social factors emerged as an aspect of the intervention that children enjoyed, it was also apparent that they experienced conflicts and difficulties with group members:

> "Tom's getting really annoying now that's the thing. That's why I don't like 'LEGO Club' because it's so annoying, Tom's always winding me up."

Many preferred building by themselves and were frustrated by the building abilities of other group members, feeling that building collaboratively made the building process slower:

> "Yes well usually when I'm building at home, it takes me about five minutes."

> "I don't like building together because, well I just naturally tend to prefer to do things on my own."

Many children commented that the Builder was their favourite role and the role of the Engineer was challenging:

> "Yeah building together, but I really really really just want to be the Builder all the time, because it's really, really fun!"

> "I didn't really like doing the describing because it took a long time because I'm not really that good at describing."

Children also said that they wanted bigger, more interesting and more challenging sets than the ones that were available in sessions, showing that children's ownership of the group and what they get to build is important for motivation:

> "I liked the really big ones, and ones that are like games. The little ones are too boring they're just too easy to build."

> "Because it could actually be more interesting to look at and play with having more complex parts."

To improve LEGO®-Based Therapy, children suggested the following things:

- Have the group more frequently. ("Do it every day, do it every Monday and Friday.")

- Change group members to avoid difficult relationships. ("The choice of people. Because if you're told the first time who you are going with you could say 'I don't like him.'")

- Improve the rewards available. ("If you get a certificate you could get two models to keep.")

- Have more variety and more complex sets to build. ("Because it could actually be more interesting to look at and play with having more complex parts.")

Brett (2013) concludes with some recommendations for the future, including increased freestyle building and naturalistic play instead of set-building, which was less motivating for this group of children. She also suggested having rewards that were more motivating, and swapping roles very frequently. It was suggested that group dynamics be considered when selecting participants and that typically developing peers should be considered as positive role models. Moreover, the importance of adequate training of staff was emphasized, especially in relation to conflict resolution.

11

Conclusion

There is little doubt that long-standing, developmentally-based deficits in social functioning create significant, life-long disability. Deficits in social perception, social interest, social responsiveness, and atypical social communication and interaction patterns have a significant impact on children, adolescents, and adults with ASC, as well as other conditions, resulting in decrements in both quality of life and adaptive functioning (Howlin *et al.* 2004; Klin *et al.* 2007; Szatmari *et al.* 2003). These deficits also have an important negative impact on vocational opportunities, which is then a major secondary impact on quality of life for the identified individual, as well as for their families, friends, and communities (Gerhardt and Holmes 1997). The cost to society as a whole is vast, and appears to be growing.

Clearly, methods of intervention that can reduce the impact of these deficits in a meaningful and sustained way are of critical importance to healthcare and educational systems, as well as to society in general and, most importantly, to the individual themselves. The LEGO®-Based Therapy approach is far from being the only social development intervention currently available to providers who work with children, adolescents, and young adults with ASC and related conditions (Luiselli *et al.* 2008; Reichow and Volkmar 2010). However, the strengths of this method are, first, the fact that it is sought out and enjoyed by the participants— they not only enjoy it, but many group members quickly express insight about the value of the group for their own social development and personal life goals. Second, there is a growing accumulation of evidence, both empirical and anecdotal, that the method not only results in fairly immediate gains (LeGoff 2004) but that these gains are typically sustained and even grow over longer periods of time (LeGoff and Sherman 2006). Finally, the LEGO®-Based Therapy methodology, presented to members as a social group, the "LEGO Club," is able to create a naturalistic social environment that encompasses three key social environments: a social activity, a work environment, and the basis for meaningful, longer-term interpersonal relationships. "LEGO Club" members don't just get to interact with each other, and learn basic rules of social politeness and social norms: they collaborate on meaningfully complex and challenging projects, and they develop friendships in the process.

The success of the "LEGO Club," and its growing international popularity, may eventually lead to gains in our understanding of social development and interpersonal relationships in general. For the time being, however, we are reasonably confident that caring and adequately trained and experienced therapists can follow this model and expect to see significant, meaningful, and potentially long-term gains in social development in all relevant domains, for children, adolescents, and young adults who would otherwise show little or no long-term improvement, or possibly regression. The difficult truth for many individuals with ASC and other internalizing conditions today is that the challenges of adolescence and early adulthood often result in worsening of social isolation, increased social avoidance and social anxiety, and decreased social self-efficacy (Howlin *et al.* 2004; Klin *et al.* 2007).

Unlike many explicitly behavioral, or cognitive-behavioral, or insight-oriented therapies, the LEGO-Based

Therapy methodology was not developed out of a particular theoretic framework or ideology. It evolved as a result of the explicit interests and strengths of the participants. As a result, the LEGO®-Based Therapy approach is a mixed form of intervention, combining individual and group approaches, as well as adult-directed, child-led, and peer-mediated approaches (Christophersen and Mortweet 2001; Dugan *et al.* 1995; Luiselli *et al.* 2008; National Research Council 2001). The interventions capitalize on the natural interests of many of these children in a construction toy system, and emphasize the enhancement of peer identification and development of social identity. The methodology is flexible enough to allow for both highly structured and adult-led methods, leading to increased child-initiated and peer-mediated activities. To date, two outcome studies have shown clinically significant positive gains in social development for children with ASC who participated.

Methods for utilizing this toy system as a remedial tool with this and other populations of children are continuing to be explored and expanded. A replication study using a randomly assigned comparison group design was successfully completed at the Autism Research Centre at Cambridge University by two of the current authors, Gómez de la Cuesta (née Owens) and Baron-Cohen (Owens *et al.* 2008), and two book chapters have also been published recently by two of the other authors (LeGoff *et al.* 2010, 2011).

While many current social intervention strategies focus on improving social reasoning (Gray 1998) or on selecting specific behaviors using behavior analytic techniques (Koegel and Koegel 1995), the LEGO-Based Therapy approach attempts to improve basic social abilities, as well as skills, and the underlying motivation or interest for engaging in social interaction, and establishing social relationships. The therapy itself is clearly engaging and motivating for the group members, but it also has many similar characteristics to both natural social situations and work environments. In large part, due to the naturalistic quality and the common elements that overlap with work and social settings, the members have shown good generalization of adaptive social functioning and communication across a range of settings (LeGoff 2004; LeGoff and Sherman 2006). That is, the method seeks to fundamentally change social development, leading to sustained and generalizable gains in social functioning.

It is the authors' belief that the benefits of an intervention are more likely to be meaningful to the extent that they are based on improvements in core social abilities, social motivation, and social identity, rather than reflecting more superficial changes in specific social behaviors. With regard to this belief, clearly there is a need for continued research on social development, as well as the methods for improving it. The authors feel that the LEGO®-Based Therapy approach is at least a step in the right direction. Finally, LEGO-Based Therapy stands in contrast to other therapies such as Applied Behavioral Analysis (ABA) in being based on intrinsic reward (the children need no persuasion to play with LEGO) rather than extrinsic reward. Most exciting for us as scientist-practitioners is the idea that LEGO-Based Therapy taps into core strengths in people with autism: their love of patterns, regularity, decomposing wholes into parts, predictability, understanding how things work, and creating variety out of structured manipulation of variables. Scientists call this collection of skills "systemizing." LEGO-Based Therapy uses such strengths in a social context, to make social learning fun and to play to the child's strengths, not their disabilities.

We do not think that LEGO-Based Therapy is the only way to harness systemizing skills in the service of learning social skills, but it is one method that the children we seek to help have drawn to our attention, over and over again, in the waiting room of the clinic, in their bedroom alone, and in the toy store. "Let us play with LEGO®" is the message coming out of their actions. We have listened. We look forward to further research in the form of large-scale randomized control trials (RCTs) to help researchers, parents, clinicians, and educators make informed choices about what intervention is helpful and for whom.

Appendix A

LEGO®-Based Therapy
Intake Assessment

Interviewer: _____ Date of Interview: _____

Identifying Information

Name: _____ Date of Birth: _____

Chronological Age: _____

Parent(s)/Guardian(s): _____

Address: _____

_____

Phone: _____

Email: _____

School/Institution: _____

Developmental Information

Actual or Estimated Full Scale IQ: ____ VIQ - ____ PIQ - ____

Adaptive Functioning:

    Language: ___ Above age level

                    ___ Age level

                    ___ Mild delay

                    ___ Moderate delay

                    ___ Severe delay

Communication: __ Above age level
                          __ Age level
                          __ Mild delay
                          __ Moderate delay
                          __ Severe delay

Social Development: __ Above age level
                          __ Age level
                          __ Mild delay
                          __ Moderate delay
                          __ Severe delay

Fine Motor: __ Above age level
                          __ Age level
                          __ Mild delay
                          __ Moderate delay
                          __ Severe delay

Gross Motor: __ Above age level
                          __ Age level
                          __ Mild delay
                          __ Moderate delay
                          __ Severe delay

Self-Help: __ Above age level
                          __ Age level
                          __ Mild delay
                          __ Moderate delay
                          __ Severe delay

Diagnosis: Axis I -   _____

                          _____

              Axis II -   _____

                          _____

              Axis III - _____

                          _____

Axis IV - _____

_____

Axis V - GAF: Current - __ Past Year High - ____

Previous or Current Treatment: _____

Medications: _____

Educational Placement: _____

Grade: _____   Supports: _____

Modifications: _____

Social Development

Friendships: _____

Peer Preferences: _____

Play Activities: _____

Autistic Features

Stigmatizing or Stereotyped Behaviors: _____

Obsessive Interests: _____

Interfering/Disruptive Behaviors: _____

Causal/Setting Events for Interfering Behaviors: _____

Causal/Setting Events for Prosocial Behavior: _____

Appendix B

Structured Observation

Building a Small Set

Does the child comply with the request appropriately and independently?

Does the child request help in completing the set or do so independently?

Does the child make eye contact and engage in other appropriate social communication in response to the interviewer?

Is the child able to complete the task easily, or with difficulty?

Is the set completed correctly?

Does the child follow the directions in a step-wise fashion, or do they jump ahead, or complete the set without following the directions?

Does the child modify the set or make something completely novel?

Does the child show the end results to the interviewer or parent(s) when done, or do they simply leave the set aside and move on?

Does the child maintain contact by verbal or nonverbal communication while building?

Freestyle Building

What is the extent and duration of preparation—that is, evidence of planning versus impulsivity?

What is the organization and structure of the results: again, is there evidence of form and planning, or is it poorly constructed and chaotic?

Is there evidence of a theme or predominant obsessive interest?

Does the child request help with either ideas or construction?

Does the child decide on a design, or do they change frequently, or change how they label or describe the creation frequently?

How long does the child sustain focus independently on this task?

Does the child show pride and request social approval following the task?

Are they able to stop when requested or do they insist on continuing to build at the end of the interview?

Do they exhibit any inappropriate behaviors related to frustration during building or in transitioning from the task?

Appendix C

LEGO®-Based Therapy
Log and Session Plan

Group Members: _____

Therapist(s): _____

Location: _____

Session Number: _____

Plan

Activities for this session (e.g. introduce rules, brick descriptions, build a particular model, give certificates, etc.)

_____

_____

_____

_____

_____

Targets for this session (e.g. children to work together, practice turn-taking, any behaviors you want to work on)

_____

_____

_____

_____

_____

Evaluation

During the session did the child... (tick the appropriate column for each statement below)

	Never or rarely	With prompting	Sometimes	Often
Build models with other children?				
Follow the LEGO® Rules?				
Use strategies for compromise and negotiation?				
Use strategies for reconciliation?				
Help other children?				
Take turns?				
Initiate conversations with other children?				
Respond to other children positively if they initiated social interactions?				
Show negative behavior (aggression, tantrums, etc.)?				
Avoid other children?				
Mock or bully other children?				
(add your own here....)				

	Never	Sometimes	Often
Praise the children?			
Highlight problems to children?			
Allow children to come up with their own solutions to social problems?			
Give time out to child?			
Prompt children to use positive social behavior (e.g. practice a strategy the children have come up with before)?			

Did the child receive a certificate? (circle)

Helper   Builder   Creator   Master   Genius

Other Comments and Observations:

_____

_____

_____

_____

_____

_____

_____

_____

_____

_____

References

Albanese, A.L., San Miguel, S.K., and Koegel, R.L. (1995) "Social support for families." In, R.L. Koegel and L.K. Koegel (eds) *Teaching children with autism: Strategies for initiating positive interactions and improving learning opportunities.* Baltimore, MD: Brookes Publishing.

American Psychiatric Association (APA) (2000) *Diagnostic and Statistical Manual of Mental Disorders, Fourth Edition.* Washington, DC: APA.

Attwood, T. (1998) *Asperger's Syndrome: A Guide for Parents and Professionals.* London: Jessica Kingsley Publishers.

Baron-Cohen, S. (1995) *Mindblindness: An essay on autism and theory of mind.* Cambridge, MA: MIT Press.

Brett, E. (2013) *LEGO® Therapy: Developing Social Competence in Children with Asperger Syndrome through Collaborative LEGO® play.* Unpublished Doctoral Thesis, submitted for the degree of Doctor of Child, Community and Educational Psychology, University of Essex, UK.

Carter, E., Cushing, L.S., Clark, N.M., and Kennedy, C.H. (2005) "Effects of peer support interventions on students' access to the general curriculum and social interactions." *Research and Practice for Persons with Severe Disabilities 30*, 1, 15–25.

Christophersen, E.R., and Mortweet, S.L. (2001) *Treatments that Work with Children: Empirically Supported Strategies for Managing Childhood Problems.* Washington, DC: American Psychological Association.

Cumine, V., Leach, J., and Stevenson, G. (1999) *Asperger Syndrome: A Practical Guide for Teachers.* London: David Fulton.

Cushing, L., and Kennedy, C. (1997) "Academic effects of providing peer support in general education classrooms on students without disabilities." *Journal of Applied Behavior Analysis 30*, 1, 139–151.

Dugan, E., Kamps, D., Leonard, B., Watkins, N., Rheinberger, A., and Stackhaus, J. (1995) "Effects of cooperative learning groups during social studies for students with autism and fourth grade peers." *Journal of Applied Behavior Analysis 28*, 175–188.

Franca, V.M., Kerr, M.M., Reitz, A.L., and Lambert, D. (1990) "Peer tutoring among behaviorally disordered students: Academic and social benefits to tutor and tutee." *Education and Treatment of Children 13*, 109–128.

Frea, W.D. (1995) "Social-communicative skills in higher-functioning children with autism." In R.L. Koegel and L. Koegel (eds) *Teaching Children With Autism.* New York, NY: Paul H. Brookes Publishing.

Freeman, B.J. (1997) "Guidelines for evaluation of intervention programs for children with autism." *Journal of Autism and Developmental Disorders 27,* 6, 641–651.

Fuchs, D., Fuchs, L.S., and Burish, P. (2000) "Peer-assisted learning strategies: An evidence-based practice to promote reading achievement." *Learning Disabilities Research and Practice 15,* 2, 85–91.

Fuchs, D., Fuchs, L.S., Mathes, P.G., and Martinez, E. (2002) "Preliminary evidence on the social standing of students with learning disabilities in PALS and No-PALS classrooms." *Learning Disabilities Research and Practice 17,* 4, 205–215.

Garber, S.W., Garber, M.D., and Spizman, R.F. (1993) *Monsters Under the Bed and Other Childhood Fears: Helping Your Child Overcome Anxiety, Fears and Phobias.* New York, NY: Villard.

Gerhardt, P.F., and Holmes, D.L. (1997) "Employment: Options and Issues for Adolescents and Adults with Autism." In D.J. Cohen and F.R. Volkmar (eds) *Handbook of Autism and Pervasive Developmental Disorders.* New York, NY: John Wiley.

Gilliam, J. (1995) *Gilliam Autism Rating Scale (GARS).* Houston, TX: Pro-Ed.

Gilliam, J. (2001) *Gilliam Asperger Disorder Scale (GADS).* Houston, TX: Pro-Ed.

Gilliam, J. (2006) *Gilliam Autism Rating Scale, Second Edition (GARS-2).* Houston, TX: Pro-Ed.

Gilliam, J. (2013) *Gilliam Autism Rating Scale, Third Edition (GARS-3).* Houston, TX: Pro-Ed.

Gray, C.A. (1994) *Comic Strip Conversations.* Arlington, TX: Future Horizons Press.

Gray, C.A. (1998) "Social Stories and Comic Strip Conversations with Students with Asperger Syndrome and High-Functioning Autism." In E. Schopler, G.B. Mesibov, and L. Kunce (eds) *Asperger Syndrome or High Functioning Autism?* New York, NY: Plenum.

Gray, C.A. (2000) *The New Social Storybook.* Arlington, TX: Future Horizons Press.

Gray, C.A., and Garand, J. (1993) "Social stories: Improving responses of individuals with autism with accurate social information." *Focus on Autistic Behavior 8,* 1–10.

Greenspan, S.I., Simons, R., and Wieder, S. (1998) *The Child with Special Needs: Encouraging Intellectual and Emotional Growth.* Reading, MA: Addison Wesley Longman.

Greenwood, C.R., Carta, J.J., and Hall, R.V. (1988) "The use of peer tutoring strategies in classroom management and educational instruction." *School Psychology Review 17,* 2, 258–275.

Greenwood, C.R., Carta, J.J., and Kamps, D. (1990) "Teacher-mediated Versus Peer-Mediated Instruction: A Review of Advantages and Disadvantages." In H.C. Foot, M.J. Morgan, and R.H. Shute (eds) *Children Helping Children.* Chichester, UK: John Wiley.

Greenwood, C.R., Hou, L.S., Delquadri, J., Terry, B., and Arreaga-Mayer, C. (2001) "The Class Wide Peer Tutoring Learning Management System (CWPT-LMS)." In J. Woodward and L. Cuban (eds) *Technology, Curriculum, and Professional Development: Adapting Schools to Meet the Needs of Students with Disabilities.* Newberry Park, CA: Corwin.

Haring, T.G., and Breen, C.G. (1992) "A peer-mediated social network intervention to enhance the social integration of persons with moderate and severe disabilities." *Journal of Applied Behavior Analysis 25*, 319–334.

Harris, S.L., and Handleman, J.S. (1997) "Helping children with autism enter the mainstream." In D.J. Cohen and F.R. Volkmar (eds) *Handbook of Autism and Pervasive Developmental Disorders, Second Edition.* New York, NY: John Wiley & Sons.

Harris, S.L., and Weiss, M.J. (1998) *Right From the Start: Behavioral intervention for young children with autism: A guide for parents and professionals.* Bethesda, MD: Woodbine House.

Heflin, L.J., and Simpson, R.L. (1998) "Interventions for children and youth with autism: Prudent choices in a world of exaggerated claims and empty promises." *Focus on Autism and Other Developmental Disabilities 13*, 4, 194–211.

Howlin, P., Goode, S., Hutton, J. and Rutter, M. (2004) "Adult outcome for children with autism." *Journal of Child Psychology and Psychiatry 45*, 2, 212–229.

Howlin, P., Hadwin, J., and Baron-Cohen, S. (1999) *Teaching Children with Autism to Mind-Read: A Practical Guide for Teachers and Parents.* New York, NY: John Wiley.

Kendall, P.C., and Hedtke, K.A. (2006) *The Coping Cat Workbook* (Second edition). Ardmore, PA: Workbook Publishing.

Klin, A., and Volkmar, F.R. (1997) "Asperger's Syndrome." In D.J. Cohen and F.R. Volkmar (eds) *Handbook of Autism and Pervasive Developmental Disorders.* New York, NY: John Wiley.

Klin, A., and Volkmar, F.R. (2000) "Treatment and Intervention Guidelines for Individuals with Asperger Syndrome." In A. Klin, F. Volkmar, and S.S. Sparrow (eds) *Asperger Syndrome.* New York, NY: Guilford.

Klin, A., Saulnier, C.A., Sparrow, S.S., Ciccehetti, D.V., Volkmar, F.R., and Lord, C. (2007) "Social and communication abilities and disabilities in higher functioning individuals with autism spectrum disorders: The Vineland and the ADOS." *Journal of Autism and Developmental Disorders 37*, 748–759.

Klin, A., Volkmar, F.R., and Sparrow, S.S. (eds) (2000) *Asperger Syndrome.* New York, NY: Guilford.

Koegel, L.K., Koegel, R.L., Hurley, C., and Frea, W.D. (1992) "Improving social skills and disruptive behavior in children with autism through self-management." *Journal of Applied Behavior Analysis 25*, 341–353.

Koegel, R.L., and Koegel, L.K. (1995) *Teaching Children with Autism.* New York, NY: Paul H. Brookes.

Kohler, F.W, Strain, P., Hoyson, M, and Jamieson, B. (1997) "Merging naturalistic teaching and peer-based strategies to address the IEP objectives of preschoolers with autism: An examination of structural and child behavior outcomes." *Focus on Autism and Other Developmental Disabilities 12*, (4), 196–206.

Kunce, L., and Mesibov, G.B. (1998) "Educational Approaches to High-Functioning Autism and Asperger Syndrome." In E. Schopler, G.B. Mesibov, and L. Kunce (eds) *Asperger Syndrome or High Functioning Autism?* New York, NY: Plenum.

Laushey, K.M., and Heflin, L.J. (2000) "Enhancing social skills of kindergarten children with autism through the training of multiple peers as tutors." *Journal of Autism and Developmental Disorders 30*, 3, 183–193.

Leaf, R., and McEachin, J. (1999) *A Work in Progress: Behavior Management Strategies and a Curriculum for Intensive Behavioral Treatment of Autism.* New York, NY: DRL Books.

LeGoff, D.B. (2004) "Use of LEGO® as a therapeutic medium for improving social competence." *Journal of Autism and Developmental Disorders 34*, 5, 557–571.

LeGoff, D.B., and Sherman, M. (2006) "Long-term outcome of social skills intervention based on interactive LEGO play." *Autism 10*, 4, 1–31.

LeGoff, D.B., Krauss, G.W., and Levin Allen, S. (2010) "LEGO® Play Therapy for Children with Autistic Disorders." In A.A. Drewes and C.E. Schaefer (eds) *School-Based Play Therapy* (Second edition). Hoboken, NJ: John Wiley.

LeGoff, D.B., Krauss, G.W., and Levin Allen, S. (2011) "Innovative Uses of LEGO® Materials for Improving Social Competence in Children and Adolescents." In L. Gallo-Lopez, and L. Rubin (eds) *Play-Based Interventions for Children and Adolescents on the Autism Spectrum.* New York: Routledge.

Licciardello, C.C., Harchik, A.E., and Luiselli, J.K. (2008) "Social skills intervention for children with autism during interactive play at a public elementary school." *Education and Treatment of Children 31*, 1, 27–37.

Luiselli, J.K., Russo, D.C., Christian, W.P., and Wilczynski, S.M. (2008) *Effective Practices for Children with Autism: Educational and Behavioral Support Interventions That Work.* Oxford, UK: Oxford University Press.

Mesibov, G.B. (1984) "Social skills training with verbal autistic adolescents and adults: A program model." *Journal of Autism and Developmental Disorders 17*, 6, 433–465.

Mesibov, G.B. (1992) "Treatment issues with high-functioning adolescents and adults with autism." In E. Schopler and G.B. Mesibov (eds) *Social Behavior in Autism.* New York, NY: Plenum Press.

Myles, B.S., and Simpson, R.L. (1998) *Asperger Syndrome: A Guide for Educators and Parents.* Houston, TX: Pro-Ed.

National Research Council (2001) *Educating Children With Autism.* Washington, DC: NRC Press.

Owens, G., Granader, Y., Humphrey, A., and Baron-Cohen, S. (2008) "LEGO® Therapy and the Social Use of Language Programme: An evaluation of two social skills interventions for children with high functioning autism and Asperger syndrome." *Journal of Autism and Developmental Disorders 38*, 10, 1944–1957.

Ozonoff, S., and Griffith, E.M. (2000) "Neuropsychological Function and the External Validity of Asperger Syndrome." In A. Klin, F. Volkmar, and S.S. Sparrow (eds) *Asperger Syndrome.* New York, NY: Guilford.

Ozonoff, S., and Miller, J.N. (1995) "Teaching Theory of Mind: A New Approach to Social Skills Training for Individuals With Autism." *Journal of Autism and Development Disorders 25*, 4, 415–433.

Pierce, K., and Schreibman, L. (1997) "Using peer trainers to promote social behavior in autism: Are they effective at enhancing multiple social modalities?" *Focus on Autism and Other Developmental Disabilities 12*, 207–218.

Quill, K. (1995) *Teaching Children with Autism: Strategies to Enhance Communication and Socialization*. New York, NY: Delmar.

Quill, K. (1997) "Instructional considerations for young children with autism: The rationale for visually cued instruction." *Journal of Autism and Developmental Disorders 27*, 697–714.

Rapee, R.M., and Heimberg, R.G. (1997) "A cognitive-behavioral model of anxiety in social phobia." *Behavior Research and Therapy 35*, 741–756.

Reichow, B., and Volkmar, F.R. (2010) "Social skills interventions for individuals with autism: Evaluation for evidence-based practices within a best evidence synthesis framework." *Journal of Autism and Developmental Disorders 40*, 2, 149–166.

Rinaldi, W. (2004) *Social Use of Language Programme. Infant and Primary School Teaching Pack*. Cranleigh: Wendy Rinaldi.

Schopler, E. (1987) "Specific and nonspecific factors in the effectiveness of a treatment system." *American Psychologist 42*, 376–383.

Schopler, E., and Mesibov, G.B. (1986) *High Functioning Individuals with Autism*. New York, NY: Plenum Press.

Schopler, E., and Mesibov, G.B. (1992) *Social Behavior in Autism*. New York, NY: Plenum Press.

Schopler, E., Mesibov, G.B., and Kunce, L.J. (1998) *Asperger Syndrome or High Functioning Autism?* New York, NY: Plenum Press.

Sparrow, S.S., Balla, D.A., and Cicchetti, D.V. (1984) *Vineland Adaptive Behavior Scales*. Circle Pines, MN: American Guidance Service.

Sparrow, S.S., Cicchetti, D.V., and Balla, D.A. (2005) *Vineland Adaptive Behavior Scales* (Second edition). San Antonio, TX: Pearson.

Steege, M., Mace, F.C., Perry, L., and Longenecker, H. (2007) "Applied behavioral analysis: Beyond discrete trial teaching." *Psychology in the Schools 44*, 1, 91–99.

Strain, P.S., and Schwartz, I. (2001) "ABA and the development of meaningful social relations for young children with autism." *Focus on Autism and Other Developmental Disabilities 16*, 120–128.

Swaggart *et al.* (1995) "Using social stories to teach social and behavioral skills to children with autism." *Focus on Autism and Other Developmental Disabilities 10*, 1, 1–16.

Szatmari, P., Bryson, S.E., Boyle, M.H., Streiner, D.L., and Duku, E. (2003) "Predictors of outcome among high functioning children with autism and Asperger Syndrome." *Journal of Child Psychology and Psychiatry 44*, 4, 520–528.

Topping, K. (1988) *The Peer Tutoring Handbook: Promoting Cooperative Learning*. Cambridge, MA: Brookline.

Weiss, M.J., and Harris, S.L. (2001) *Reaching Out, Joining In: Teaching social skills to young children with autism*. Bethesda, MD: Woodbine House.

Whitaker, P., Barratt, P., Joy, H., Potter, M., and Thomas, G. (1998) "Children with autism and peer group support: using 'circles of friends'." *British Journal of Special Education 25*, 2, 60–64.

Subject Index

Author Index

American Psychiatric
 Association (APA) 21
Attwood, T. 11, 13, 14

Balla, D.A. 23, 106, 107
Baron-Cohen, S. 12, 15
Breen, C.G. 29
Brett, E. 114, 117
Burish, P. 29

Carta, J.J. 29
Carter, E. 29
Christophersen, E.R. 11,
 53, 121
Cicchetti, D.V. 23, 106,
 107
Cumine, V. 13
Cushing, L. 29

Dugan, E. 29, 121

Franca, V.M. 29
Frea, W.D. 12
Freeman, B.J. 13
Fuchs, D. 29
Fuchs, L.S. 29

Garand, J. 12
Garber, M.D. 11
Garber, S.W. 11
Gerhardt, P.F. 119
Gilliam, J. 23, 106
Gray, C.A. 12, 121
Greenspan, S.I. 14
Greenwood, C.R. 29
Griffith, E.M. 12

Hadwin, J. 15
Hall, R.V. 29
Handleman, J.S. 13, 14
Harchik, A.E. 11, 12
Haring, T.G. 29

Harris, S.L. 12, 13, 14
Hedtke, K.A. 11
Heflin, L.J. 14, 29
Heimberg, R.G. 11
Holmes, D.L. 119
Howlin, P. 12, 15, 119,
 120

Kamps, D. 29
Kendall, P.C. 11
Kennedy, C. 29
Klin, A. 11, 12, 13, 119,
 120
Koegel, L.K. 13, 14, 37,
 121
Koegel, R.L. 12, 13, 14,
 37, 121
Kohler, F.W. 29
Krauss, G.W. 11, 24, 121
Kunce, L.J. 13, 17

Laushey, K.M. 14, 29
Leach, J. 13
Leaf, R. 37, 43
LeGoff, D.B. 9, 11, 21, 23,
 24, 106, 120, 121,
 122
Levin Allen, S. 11, 24,
 121
Licciardello, C.C. 11, 12
Luiselli, J.K. 11, 12, 13,
 119, 121

McEachin, J. 37, 43
Mesibov, G.B. 12, 13, 17
Miller, J.N. 12
Mortweet, S.L. 11, 53,
 121
Myles, B.S. 13

National Research Council
 13, 121

Owens, G. 9, 24, 121
Ozonoff, S. 12

Pierce, K. 14, 44

Quill, K. 12, 13

Rapee, R.M. 11
Reichow, B. 11, 13, 119
Rinaldi, W. 24

San Miguel, S.K. 12
Schopler, E. 12, 13
Schreibman, L. 14, 44
Schwartz, I. 11, 12
Sherman, M. 9, 23, 106,
 120, 122
Simons, R. 14
Simpson, R.L. 13, 14
Sparrow, S.S. 13, 23, 106,
 107
Spizman, R.F. 11
Steege, M. 37
Stevenson, G. 13
Strain, P.S. 11, 12
Swaggart, B.L. 12
Szatmari, P. 119

Topping, K. 29

Volkmar, F.R. 11, 12, 13,
 119

Weiss, M.J. 12, 13
Whitaker, P. 29
Wieder, S. 14